The Alpine 4000m Peaks
by the Classic Routes

Richard Goedeke

The Alpine 4000m Peaks
by the Classic Routes

Descriptions of the standard ascents of all the
4000-metre peaks in the Alps, with 48 black/white
and 48 colour photographs, 32 sketch maps and 17 topos.

Edited from an original translation by Jill Neate

Diadem Books · London
Menasha Ridge Press · Birmingham, Alabama

Cover photograph: On the Hornli Ridge of the Matterhorn.
Frontispiece: On the Summit Ridge of the Aiguille Verte.
Photograph on page 7: Matterhorn from NW from the Wandfluesattel.
Photograph on page 12: View from Lagginhorn eastwards towards the Bernina.

Picture credits (page numbers): Gran 70, 80, 145, 163.
Rauschel 29, 33, 35, 38, 47, 51, 61, 87, 109, 131, 134, 135, 142, 143, 207, 211.

All other photographs as well as the sketch maps an topos
by the author.

Copyright of the original German edition © 1990 by Verlag J. Berg, München
Copyright in English translation © 1991 by Diadem Books, London

Published simultaneously in UK an USA by Diadem Books, London

All trade enquiries UK and Commonwealth to:
Hodder and Stoughton, Mill Road, Dunton Green, Sevenoaks, Kent TN13 2YA

All trade enquiries in USA to:
Menasha Ridge Press, 3169 Cahaba Heights Road, Birmingham, Alabama 35243

British Library Cataloguing-in-Publication Data:
Goedeke, Richard
The Alpine 4000m peaks by classic routes.
I. Title 796.5

All rights reserved.

Library of Congress Cataloguing-in-Publication Data:
Goedeke, Richard, 1939–
[4000er, die Normalwege. English]
The Alpine 4000m peaks by the classic routes: a guide for mountaineers /
Richard Goedeke: edited from an original translation
by Jill Neate.
p. cm.
Translation of: 4000er, die Normalwege.
"Descriptions of the standard ascents of all the 4000-metre peaks in the Alps, with 48 black/white and 48 colour photographs, 32 sketch maps an 17 topos."
Includes bibliographical references and index.

ISBN 3-7634-1007-4
1. Mountaineering—Alps—Guide-books. 2. Alps—Description and ravel—Guide-books.
I. Neate, Jill. II. Title. III. Title: GV199.44.A4G6413 1991
796.5'22'094947—dc20
91–21684 CIP

Printed in Germany

Preface

The 4000ers are terrific. Quite beautifully big. Quite beautifully cold. Quite beautifully wild. Even though the heights look modest by comparison with high peaks on other continents, the 4000ers of the Alps rise further above the snow-line than many much higher mountains in the Himalaya and in the Andes. And to climb them, one need neither contribute to the hole in the ozone layer with long-distance flights nor diminish one's savings. Furthermore, one does not have to make excessive demands on one's normal professional and family life. No wonder, therefore, that many people collect 4000ers.

The ordinary routes on these peaks are considerable challenges. Above all, however, they are the most logical routes, for they trace the lines of least resistance, were mostly the routes of first ascent, and thereby remain a part of classical Alpine history. To take note of this history, gives additional dimensions of experience to our ascents today. And even though these routes receive heavy traffic they renew themselves constantly with fresh snow. Changes in circumstances, usually in the weather, add an extra degree of unpredictability and often produce surprising problems that can lead to a change of route. That is all part of the fascination of big mountains, which makes the ordinary routes perennially interesting even for those who normally tackle harder climbs.

So, why this guidebook? There are already so many. There are also beautiful, thick books, of large format, with many colourful pictures, on highly glazed paper, heavy, voluminous, and much too good to carry around. Hence this little pocket book which is, nonetheless, readable without a magnifying glass, perhaps even by the light of a candle or head lamp.

For that reason we have omitted the text-book references. Naturally, all those who climb the 4000ers will already know that in the Western Alps the hut climb is often more exacting than a full mountain excursion in the Eastern Alps. In addition, the critical importance of good Alpine technique cannot be overstressed.

Fitness and acclimatization are also very important prerequisites, requiring a sensible tactical plan to acquire them. Then we need settled weather and favourable conditions for the type of climb being tackled, together with a suitably early start to allow it to be completed in relative safety. Finally good equipment with ample food and fuel are needed. All these factors need to be present to ensure success.

This is not an alpine instruction book. However, we trust that collectors of 4000ers will take care to equip themselves properly before embarking on these climbs, otherwise, they will not get far with their 4000m peak collecting.

This guide gives sufficient information so that, apart from the appropriate detailed maps, no further references are necessary. I have also provided details of how to get to the departure points by public transport which, as everybody knows, is more environmentally friendly than the motor car. [Editor's note: the author is a member of the West German Green Party.]

The guidebook was prepared from the basis of several decade's experience in these mountains. For that purpose I thank all those who have supported me in so doing, with word and deed, above all Heinrich Bauregger, Gotlind Blechschmidt, Hartmut Eberlein, Klaus-Jürgen Gran, Andreas Hartmann, Susanne Hornburg, Joachim Linde, Helmut Krämer, Axel Naujoles, Wolfgang Rauschel, Hans Steinbichler and Thomas Stephan. The need for a second edition has given an opportunity to incorporate the results of further investigations and to deal with some corrections. If there should still be errors or changes on the mountain that lead to an important new route direction, I shall be grateful for letters which can help to improve further editions. To all who use this guidebook, I wish you much joy and a safe return.

Braunschweig, 1991   Richard Goedeke

Address: Dr. Richard Goedeke, Liebermannstr. 4, D-3300 Braunschweig, Germany

Contents

Preface 5

Notes – including mountain rescue 10

The big isolated peaks
Piz Bernina 13, Gran Paradiso 18, Barre des Écrins 21

Central Bernese Oberland
Aletschhorn 25, Jungfrau 30, Mönch 34, Gross-Fiescherhorn 36, Hinter-Fiescherhorn 38, Gross-Grünhorn 39

Eastern Bernese Oberland
Schreckhorn 42, Lauteraarhorn 45, Finsteraarhorn 50

Pennine Alps 53
Eastern Pennine Alps – Weissmies group
Lagginhorn 54, Weissmies 58

Northern Pennine Alps – Mischabel
Dürrenhorn 60, Hohberghorn 60, Stecknadelhorn 60, Nadelhorn 60, 64, Lenzspitze 82, Dom 85, Täschhorn 88

Northern Pennine Alps – Allalin group
Alphubel 91, Allalinhorn 95, Rimpfischhorn 99, Strahlhorn 103

North-Western Pennine Alps
Bishorn 105, Weisshorn 107, Zinalrothorn 111, Obergabelhorn 115, Dent Blanche 117

Eastern Pennine frontier crest – Monte Rosa group
Nordend 120, Dufourspitze 123, Zumsteinspitze 127, Signalkuppe 128, Parrotspitze 131, Ludwigshöhe 132, Schwarzhorn 133, Balmenhorn 133, Vincent Piramide 134

Contents

Central Pennine frontier crest
Liskamm 136, Castor 139, Pollux 141, Breithorn 143,
Matterhorn 162, Dent d'Hérens 169

Western Pennine frontier crest
Grand Combin 171

Eastern Mont Blanc region
Aiguille Verte 176, Grande Rocheuse 183, Aiguille du Jardin 184,
Les Droites 185, Grandes Jorasses 187, Dôme de Rochfort 192,
Aiguille de Rochfort 192, Dent du Géant 195

Mont Blanc Massif
Mont Blanc du Tacul 197, Mont Maudit 201, Mont Blanc 205,
Aiguille de Bionnassay 217, Mont Brouillard 219, Punta
Baretti 219, Aiguille Blanche 222

Further reading 229

Tables
All 4000ers of the Alps by height 230
The 4000ers organised into their grading categories 234
How much sweat? Least ascent by ordinary route 236

Index 238

A Note on Rock Climbing Grades and Training 240

Notes

Under **Difficulties** is given first the overall difficulty, followed by the actual climbing difficulties, also length, rock quality, altitude and seriousness of the route. The abbreviations used represent the French designations customary in the Western Alps:

F	facile	easy
PD	peu difficile	not very hard
AD	assez difficile	fairly hard
D	difficile	hard
TD	très difficile	very hard
ED	extrêmement difficile	extremely hard

After that, the climbing difficulties on dry rock are given according to the UIAA scale (e.g. III+) and for ice and snow the maximum steepness in degrees (e.g. 50°) are given. Remember that the difficulty of rock-climbs can change considerably under snow and ice; likewise, bear in mind that it makes an enormous difference on snow or ice whether there is an established track or line of steps.

Under **Dangers**, only objective dangers are mentioned. Naturally, anyone can lose his life very quickly on objectively safe sections as well, if he assesses the weather or his own ability wrongly or botches his equipment, or makes an error in technique. Another factor to take into consideration is the danger when climbing below another group of climbers, either from falling stones or ice clips, or worse, falling climbers. (There have been several very catastrophic accidents of this type.)

Other References: In descriptions, 'right' and 'left' are used in the sense of the principal direction of travel. Abbreviations:

B	beds (e.g.Matratzenlager)
LKS	Landeskarte der Schweiz (Swiss map series)
m	metre
mH	height gain in metres
N,S,E,W.	north, south, east, west
orogr.	orographically, seen in direction of flow
hrs.	hours (average going time)
SAC/CAF/CAI	Swiss/French/Italian Alpine Club
Tel.	telephone number (not guaranteed)

The descriptions were drawn up on the basis that a guidebook is only be a general aid to route-finding and not a finite instruction. On the high peaks, the range of possible changes according to previous and current weather conditions is considerable. To judge where best to go in detail in the given conditions remains the task for all who climb. Such judgements also involve knowing when to turn back; the mountains will still be there for future attempts. If, nevertheless, despite all circumspection, we get into difficulties:

Alpine Distress Signal

Six times in a minute a visible or audible sign. Reply, that message has been understood, *three times per minute*. Signal to helicopter with one arm: means "No, do not land, we do not require anything". Both arms above the head means "Help! Please land".

Directions for Helicopter Rescue

1. For the landing site, a horizontal place (no hollows!) of 30 x 30m is required; in the surrounding area, there should be no obstacles up to 100m radius.

2. Before landing, remove objects which can be whirled into the air by the suction of the approaching helicopter.

3. The approaching helicopter is directed, back to the wind, by a person in 'Yes' position (both arms stretched high).

4. One may only approach the grounded helicopter from in front and on a signal from the pilot.

Helicopter Rescue Alarm REGA Tel. 01-383-11-11

When reporting an accident, the following details are important: name, location, telephone number, when and what happened, type of injury/illness; exact location (co-ordinates), weather in accident area, obstacles in accident area (e.g. cables, lines). All patrons of the Swiss Air Rescue Service REGA receive free rescue service inside Switzerland. (Swiss Air Rescue Service, Mainaustrasse 21, CH-8008 Zurich, Tel. 01-385-85-85; annual subscription currently about £9.00 or $16.00. Family subscriptions are available.)

Apart from the three highest mountain chains, which contain most of the peaks rising above four thousand metres, there are three lower ranges in which, in each case, only the highest summit achieves the requisite height. Nevertheless, these are quite independent massifs and the mountains of all three underline, by their originality and form, how foolish it would be if one's only criterion in the choice of goal were merely the fascination of height. But it is the 4000m peaks that concern us here:

Piz Bernina, 4049m

Along the strikingly straight valley furrow of the Engadine, the Bernina Alps rise above the magic height on the icily brilliant Piz Bernina. Whether this 'Ballroom of the Alps', as Walter Flaig called them, is the most easterly group of the Western Alps or the most westerly of the Eastern Alps, belongs to the arcane discussions of the categorizers. Also, the dry statement that this, after Mont Blanc, is the most independent elevation in the Alps, taken at face value means little. The main point is that this splendid mountain massif, in the elegance of its lines and impact of its bulk, is one of the most architecturally appealing mountains in the Alps; offering a refreshing change from the more dominant ranges further to the west.

The first ascent was made in 1850 by the Swiss surveyor Johann Coaz and the brothers Jon and Lorenz Ragut Tscharner taking a route up the long Morteratsch Glacier to the Fuorcla Crast'Aguzza and from there up the South Ridge. The celebrated Biancograt (in Romansh, Crast'Alva) leads to the summit from the north and was first climbed complete in 1876 (to Pte. Alva) by Henri Cordier and Thomas Middlemore with their guides J. Juan and K. Maurer. The final stretch to the summit was added by Paul Güssfeldt and party two years later.

Difficulties: PD. Predominantly a glacier route with long and complicated approaches to the hut below the final summit ridge (pitches of II and I) which are made easier (but not beautified) by fixed ropes.

Effort: The hut climb to the Marco e Rosa Hut from the Diavolezza Hut is 1050mH (5-6 hrs), from Morteratsch via the Boval Hut 600mH + 1100mH (2-3 + 4-6 hrs), from Franscia via the Marinelli Hut 1250mH + 1000mH (4 + 3-4 hrs). Summit climb 500mH (2 hrs) from the Marco e Rosa Hut.

Dangers: On all glacier ascents to the Fuorcla Crast'Agüzza, especially from the north, there are many crevasses and occasionally also the possibility of avalanches. The least dangerous approach is from the Diavolezza. On the narrow summit ridge beware of cornices. In a crowd, discipline and circumspection on meeting and overtaking manoeuvres is important, especially on the ascent of the Biancograt. In poor visibility, particularly if the track is lost, there are considerable route-finding problems on the Morteratsch Glacier. In bad weather the descent from the Marco e Rosa Hut can be arduous. This is true both of the wire ropes (severe danger from lightning in thunder storm) on the Italian side, and of the glaciers on the north side when the risks of crevasse falls in new snow are increased.

Pleasures: The highest summit of the Eastern Alps with splendid views of the adjacent Bernina peaks.

Maps: LKS 1277 Piz Bernina 1:25,000, also LKS 44 Maloja 1:100,000 series.

Travel: By rail via Zürich-Chur-St Moritz or by car through the long valley of the Engadine to *Pontresina* (1805m, tourist resort summer and winter, also youth hostel, Tel. 082-67 223) and Bernina railway to Hotel Morteratsch (1896m, 6km from Pontresina); valley station of the Diavolezza cableway at Bernina-Suot (2093m, 10km from Pontresina). On the Italian side, by rail to Sondrio in the Val Tellina 23km and by car through the Val Malenco to Franscia (1565m, mountain village), possibly as far as lower reservoir Lago di Gera (1996m).

Hut climbs: From the well-appointed *Diavolezza Hut* (2973m, private, 170 B, managed from June to September and December to April, Tel. 082-66 205), descend path south-westwards to cross (in the same direction) the Vadret Pers Glacier. On its west bank work up south to pass under the rocks of the Chamuotsch Hut, following the usually (in good weather) broad track, and then move up steeper snow slopes to the broad ridge of the Fortezzagrat.

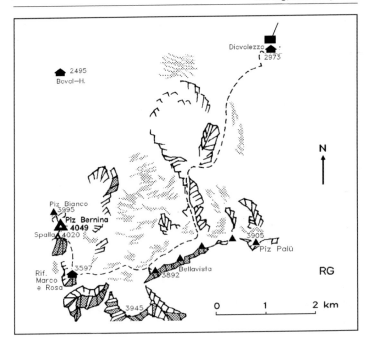

Continue along the narrowing ridge (pitches of II and I) and a steeper step, which can be turned on the west side, to reach a snow slope. Climb this to the Bellavista terraces. Before reaching the notch of the Fuorcla Bellavista, turn right and traverse westwards and south-westwards on the snow terraces, staying at about the same height, as far as north of the most westerly Bellavista summit (at the 'Eck' [corner], in sight of the prominent spire of the Crast'Agüzza). Descend steeply (big crevasses) into the uppermost snow trough of the Morteratsch Glacier. Before reaching the ice-falls, descend further to about 3600m and then traverse westwards to the flat saddle of the Fuorcla Crast'Agüzza. In the same direction and at the same height, traverse another 300m to the rocky shoulder with the two *Marco e Rosa De Marchi Huts* (3597m and 3609m, CAI, 45 B, often overcrowded, managed from July to mid-September, Tel. 0342-21 23 70).

From Morteratsch, a path takes the western moraine of the Morteratsch Glacier to reach (2 hrs) the *Boval Hut* (2495m, SAC, 100 B, managed from June to October as well as Easter and Whitsun, Tel. 082-66 403). From here, first of all cross the Morteratsch Glacier eastwards to the foot of the rocky Fortezzagrat. Along the foot of the rocks as far as the height of the rock island P.3087 on the glacier. Cross over to the right (west) towards this rock island, to a small plateau (Schnaps-bodeli). From here between the Fortezzagrat (left) and another ridge with séracs (right), climb straight up southwards to the Bellavista terraces, where the Diavolezza route is joined.

One can also climb up to the Fortezzagrat from further below on the left and ascend this (somewhat time-consuming but avoiding the glacier) to reach the Bellavista terraces. Two other (heavily crevassed) ascents lead further west through the ice-falls of the 'Buuch' and of the 'Labyrinth' respectively, directly up to the Forcella Crast'Agüzza.

The approach from the Italian side, *from Franscia* (1556m) heads north-west up the marked path to the Scerscen Hut (1813m) and continues northwards, crossing the valley to the Alpe Campascio (1844m). Climb north-east through the wood to the Alpe Musella (2021m). Continue in the same direction, over the increasingly sparse ground up to the Bocchetta delle Forbici to the *Carate Hut* (2636m, CAI). Go round the North-West Spur of the Cime di Musella to a lake under the little glacier Vedretta di Caspoggio Glacier and continue, with a right-left bend, to the *Marinelli Hut* which lies on a rock ridge (2813m, c.50 B, managed in summer). From there, head north-eastwards near the hut ridge, over debris and snow to the Passo Marinelli occidentale (3087m) which lies above the ridge. Pass northwards under the rocky spur of Piz Argient to the upper Vedretta di Scerscen Glacier. Cross this in the same direction to the foot of the rocks of Crast'Agüzza. Move under these and pass the ice or snow couloir descending from the Fuorcla Crast'Agüzza (crevasses) to the northern boundary spur of the couloir. Cross the bergschrund and climb rocks (equipped with wire ropes) to gain the Marco e Rosa Hut.

Summit climb by the Spallagrat: From the hut head northwards over the steepening snow slope to the rocks of the south-eastwards orientated ridge. Follow this (II, fixed rope), up to the fore-summit (Spalla). From whence a narrow snow ridge with one rock section (pitch of II) leads to the summit of Piz Bernina.

Piz Bernina from the north with the Bellavista terraces (top left) above the Morteratsch Glacier and the Biancograt leading up to the summit on the right.

View: To the south-west are Piz Bernina's two impressive neighbouring peaks Piz Scerscen and Piz Roseg, to the north Piz Morteratsch, to the east Piz Palü and to the south-east Piz Zupo. In addition there are also magnificent views north-westwards down to the Tschierva Glacier and north-eastwards down to the Morteratsch Glacier.

Adjacent peaks: The southern fore-summit, the **Spalla** (in Romansh, La Spedla, **4020m**) is prominent but not very independent. The northern summit, Piz Bianco (in Romansh, Piz Alb, also Piz Alv, 3995m), marks the end of the Biancograt proper, from which the main summit can only be reached via the airy and not easy connecting ridge (III in places).

Other worthwhile routes: *Biancograt* AD, this is so famous that the crowds often remove the pleasure of an otherwise magnificent excursion (pitches of III), mixed, snow or ice up to 50°. Approached from the Tschierva Hut 1450mH (7-8 hrs) of which 600mH (4 hrs) from the Forcella Prievlusa is the ridge itself.

Guidebook: Bernina Alps (West Col, 1986).

Gran Paradiso, 4061m

This is the highest summit of the Graian Alps which lie between Mont Blanc to the north and Dauphiné to the south. It is not prominent from the closer valleys, being hidden behind its surrounding mountains. Only from distant summits is its impact obvious. The name arouses concepts of a tremendous unscathed world. This atmosphere is easily imagined in this area with its dreamy cirque lakes and lonely scree ridges and snows, with the occasional view of one of the prehistoric-seeming herds of ibex. However, although this quality can be discovered around the peak it is singularly absent in the valleys and on the ordinary route of the mountain – a popularity ensured by the 'National Park' publicity tag. What one finds on the peak is a busy, well-trodden track up one of the 'easy' 4000ers. This reputation guarantees its ascent by climbers with a wider age range than is usual on mountains of this height.

Despite the popularity its ascent is far from effortless. It demands over 2000m of height-gain from the wastes of the car-park at Pont to the summit, and all of this must be made on foot. The first ascent was made by J.J. Cowell and W. Dundas with the guides J. Payot and J. Tairraz in 1860, and of course they did not have the Vittorio Emmanuele II Hut. This hut was named to commemorate the saviour of the Alpine ibex and founder of the national park.

Difficulties: PD–. As far as the summit ridge this is a rather monotonous rubble and snow plod, mostly on a broad, worn and shapeless track, with a slope of 35°, which can become icy later in the year. The final metres to the summit call for some exposed rock work (II and I).

Effort: Hut climb 700mH (2-3 hrs), summit climb 1350mH (4-5 hrs). Crossing the rubble slope of big blocks immediately behind the hut in the dark is really troublesome. The climb can also be unpleasant on account of the crowds at the hut, during the ascent, and on the summit.

Dangers: Small crevasses occasionally appear on the glacier but otherwise there is little objective danger.

However, in bad visibility or storms, because of the scale and height of the mountain, very rapid and dramatic developments are possible.

Pleasures: In contrast to those peaks which have been made docile and palatable to consumers by means of cableways, the Gran Paradiso gives the satisfaction of a high peak gained solely by personal effort. Especially impressive is the view, which suddenly develops on the approach to the summit, with fine aspects on all sides after a rather monotonous ascent.

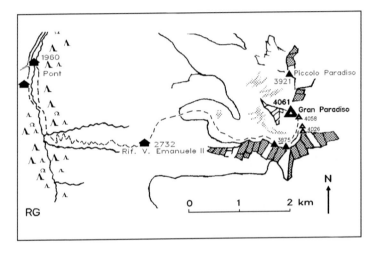

Maps: IGC 1:50,000 No.62003 Gran Paradiso; Kompass-Karte No.86 Gran Paradiso.

Travel: By rail through the Aosta valley to Sarre, 6km west of Aosta. By bus over the little road branching off the main road at Villeneuve, 11km west of Aosta, 25km southwards through the Val Savaranche up to *Pont* (1945m, hotel, camping, big car-park).

Hut climb: From Pont take the broad path up the valley and soon cross down to a stream descending in waterfalls on the left (east). Then ascend the valley slope in wide bends through the wood. Continue over sparse pastures and moraines to the *Vittorio Emmanuele II Hut*, built in the form of a half barrel (2775m; CAI, 143 B, winter room with

19

43 B, mostly overcrowded, managed from the end of April to 25 September, Tel. 0165-95 710).

Summit climb by the West Face: From the hut, head northwards over the 'block field' (tiring stumbling in the dark) to the moraines below the Gran Paradiso Glacier. Follow this and then, by way of a small valley, climb over snow to the glacier tongue. Ascend the glacier, keeping right, and at its upper part climb a steeper ice slope on the left of a block ridge (one can avoid the ice by ascending the ridge, but beware of loose blocks) to a flatter ridge. Continue to ascend this. Further on, it narrows (Eselsrücken) and leads along the edge of the glacier to the saddle in front of the pinnacle Becco del Moncorvé, towering up on the right at the edge of the south cliff. Now ascend northwards over the steeper slopes, below the rock ridge of the 'Roc' to the bergschrund. Cross this (usually without problems) and up a short rocky ridge, with a final surprisingly exposed section (I) to gain the fore-summit (Madonna). The highest point, which lies behind at the north-west end of the summit ridge, may be reached by more climbing (II and I) in about 15 minutes.

View: To the north-west the Mont Blanc massif can be seen, to the north-east the Pennine Alp frontier crest, to the south-west the Dauphiné with the Barre des Écrins and to the south Monte Viso. There is a fine view down the East Face.

Adjacent peaks: The **Madonna summit (c.4058m)** is only a little lower than the highest point. The **Central Summit (c.4015m)**, also crowned with several rock pinnacles, is quickly and easily climbed from the ordinary route (II and I). The same goes for the somewhat more difficult (II) **East Summit (II Roc 4026m)** rising on the connecting ridge. The **Piccolo Paradiso (3923m)** rises on the ridge running northwards from the main summit.

Other worthwhile routes: *East Face* (AD, II, mixed and 50°; 900mH from the Pol Bivouac).

North-West Face (D, ice or snow 50°, 600mH from the foot of the face).

North Ridge intégral (D, IV and III, 1700mH, 15 hrs from the Leonessa Bivouac).

Guidebook: Graians East (West Col, 1969).

Barre des Écrins, 4101m

In the Haut Dauphiné, far to the south-west, the Alps reach up into more rarefied air, in a row of impressive mountains. Unfortunately some of the most beautiful lie just under 4000m and the Barre des Écrins alone towers above this level. But the satellites of the majestic Barre are the essential parts of this splendid ensemble of pinnacle ridges and gloomy ice walls high above the glaciers. Anyone who scorns the peaks which fall below the critical height out of a purely superficial hunt for superlatives, has only himself to blame for the loss of many delightful experiences. Almost the entire high mountain region of the massif is a national park and thus, it is to be hoped, permanently protected from the building of téléphériques. Thus, this untouched scenery can be experienced only by those prepared to climb from the valley under their own steam. It is nevertheless continually threatened, as are many other areas of Europe, by accidents in the atomic reactors installed in the Rhône valley just west of Grenoble. The first ascent of the Barre in 1864 fell to A.W. Moore and Edward Whymper, led by Michel Croz from Chamonix (later to fall on descent after the first ascent of the Matterhorn) and the Swiss guide Christian Almer. They busied themselves in delicate step cutting up the North Face and the upper part of the East Ridge and, on descent, cleaned up the then very unstable West Ridge, over which today's ordinary route leads. Whymper's account of it in his classic book, *Scrambles Amongst the Alps*, still makes fascinating reading. The rugged South Face was climbed in 1880 by H. Duhamel and the local guides Pierre Gaspard and his son. The ascent of the overwhelming line of the South Pillar, towering above the Glacier Noir the summit, fell to the extreme climbers Jean and Jeanne Franco in 1944.

Difficulties: PD+. On the summit ridge, exposed climbing on good, stabilized rock, with pitches of II, mostly I. Otherwise a glacier climb with snow up to 40°. The bergschrund at the Brèche Lory can be troublesome.

Effort: Hut climb 1350mH from the Cézanne Hut (5 hrs), summit climb 1000mH (4 hrs).

Dangers: On some parts of the lower glacier, there is a mild danger from falling ice and some of the crevasses in the upper section should be treated with respect. Otherwise, an objectively safe ascent. Nevertheless, one should not get caught by storm high on the mountain.

Pleasures: The ascent from the bottoms of the valleys through the unspoiled scenery of the Écrins Nature Park 'creates, in its consistency and gradually impinging impressions, the pre-conditions for an especially profound and fascinating mountain experience'.

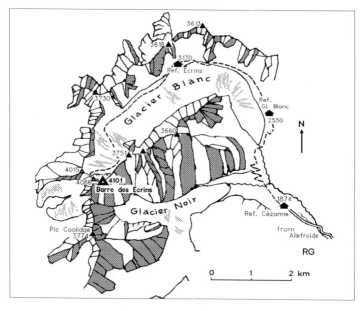

Maps: IGN 241 Massif des Écrins, Meije, Pelvoux 1:25,000, also IGN itinéraires pedestres et á ski 6, Ecrins et Haut Dauphiné 1:50,000.

Travel: By rail from the south via Gap through the valley of the Durance to l'Argentière-la-Bessée (16km south of Briançon) or from Italy via Turin and Susa to Oulx and then by bus via Col de Montgenèvre to Briançon and l'Argentière-la-Bessé. This can also be reached from the west by bus from Grenoble railway station via Col du Lautaret and Briançon. By car, by the motorways from Paris and Switzerland to Grenoble, then highway N91 over the Col du Lautaret or, from the Po plain, motorway to Turin and then highway E13 via Susa-Oulx-Col du Montgenèvre to Briançon and south to *l'Argentière-la-Bessé* (979m). From there, by bus 18km to Ailefroide (1503m, mountain village overrun with hotels; camping Tel. 9223-3200).

Hut climb: *From Ailefroide*, near the valley bottom, take a path for 5km, first of all on the asphalt road then, cutting off its bends, up to the *Cézanne Hut* (1874m, hotel, acres of car-parks, usually an awful lot of people).

Barre des Écrins from the north-east with the Refuge des Écrins on the spur on the right.

Cross over the fields of debris to the bridge over the outflow from the Glacier Noir. After that, take the grassy slope on the right in bends, over a rock-studded spur and traverse to the tongue of the Glacier Blanc. Move up over the polished rocks on the right (east) of the glacier (on an ugly steel staircase with railings), past the ruins of the old Tuckett Hut, and northwards to the *Glacier Blanc Hut* (2550m, 2-3 hrs from the Cézanne Hut; CAF, c.100 B, managed, often less crowded than the Écrins Hut!). Continue 2km up along the edge of the glacier to a rock spur (P.3016). Beyond this climb right in an arc to the already visible *Écrins Hut*, high above the glacier (3170m, CAF, 100 B, managed in summer and spring and in good weather generally bursting at the seams).

Summit climb by the North Face and West Ridge: From the Écrins Hut go down to the glacier to join the route ascending direct from the Glacier Blanc Hut. Continue to ascend, on the northern edge of the glacier, to the proximity of the Col des Écrins, sunk between the Roche Faurio (north) and the Barre des Écrins (south). Before reaching the rock towers of the Clochetons de Bonne Pierre climb (with despatch), obliquely left up the steep, avalanche-scarred slope which is threatened by the séracs above. Then follow a (usually distinct) track in the direction of P.3791 on the east ridge of the Barre, and when close under the bergschrund, traverse to the right along a slightly inclined terrace to the Brèche Lory (3974m, left of the snow top of the Dôme de Neige). Cross the bergschrund and at first ascend the steep, mixed face to gain the exposed, narrow ridge (II, unpleasant when icy) which leads up to Pic Lory. After crossing a notch on the narrowing and more exposed ridge head up to the easternmost and highest point of the mountain.

View: To the east and north far below is the impressive Glacier Blanc, and to the south the Glacier Noir. Behind that are the Pelvoux and the Ailefroide, and to the south-west Les Bans, to the north the Roche Faurio and beyond that the Meije.

Adjacent peaks: The very obvious **Pic Lory (4086m)** was crossed during the ascent. This is the connecting point between the ridge running west-north-west to the Brèche Lory and the steep ridge running south-west to the Col des Avalanches. The **Dôme de Neige (4015m)** can be climbed very quickly from the Brèche Lory.

Other worthwhile routes: *East Ridge* (AD, III and II, mixed, snow to 50°, 450mH and 2 hrs from the Brèche des Écrins).

South Face (AD, rock with longer passages of III and II, mixed, snow to 55°, from the Temple Hut 1700mH and 6-8 hrs, of that 630mH and 3-4 hrs from the Col des Avalanches).

South Pillar (TD, IV+, with passages of V+, is a splendid classic Alpine route, serious because of the lack of escape possibilities, 1100mH and 6-9 hrs from foot of face).

Guidebooks: Écrins Massif (The Alpine Club, 1987).

The Bernese Alps are not the highest mountains of the Alps but they lie on the weather or windward side, with tremendous, steep flanks facing out over the foothills. That causes especially heavy precipitation that feeds enormous glaciers. Both of the longest glaciers in the Alps are thus to be found here. To the north a high altitude railway offers a comfortable spring-board to some of the most prominent summits. But apart from that, the approaches to the peaks are long and arduous.

Aletschhorn, 4195m

The mighty pyramid of the second highest summit in the Bernese Alps dominates, with the hanging glaciers of its North Face, the snow basin of the largest ice stream in the Alps. On the vast expanses of the Grosser Aletsch Glacier, it is still possible to view a relic of the Ice Age to remind us of when such ice masses pushed themselves through all the big Alpine valleys and reached to the foothills. Even the arid and rockier southern flanks of the mountains are still framed by glaciers, studded in their lower parts with the tell-tale debris of the varying rock bands scoured by this great glacier and its feeder streams.

Today's ordinary routes on this mountain, offer a choice of difficulties, either on the glacier or on the rock. In the first case, there is the approach used in 1859 by the first climbers, Francis Tuckett, J.J. Bennen, P. Bohren and Victor Tairraz over the Mittelaletsch Glacier and the North-East Ridge. This is also the customary route for ski ascents. On the other hand, if steeper rock-climbing is required, as opposed to snow and ice, then the ascent of the South-West Face is recommended; this was opened up in 1879 by L. Lichti, A. Kummer and a porter, but may have been climbed five years earlier by T. Middlemore and party. Together they provide a large-scale traverse. A somewhat harder, but still more splendid traverse is offered by the ascent of the stylish Hasler Rib, on the left side of the North Face to the North-East Ridge. This was climbed fully to the summit by G.A. Hasler and party in 1902 (earlier ascents: in 1875 by T. Middlemore — disputed, and in 1888 by C. Luscher and party — rib only)

In all cases, because of its size and the diversity of its demands, the ascent of the Aletschhorn remains an all round alpine undertaking.

Difficulties: North-East Ridge (PD. On the erratically disrupted Mittelaletsch Glacier with its ever changing conditions, then by a snow ridge and slopes up to 40°, with, on the summit ridge, some metres of rock with climbing to I).

South-West Face (PD+ with longer passages of rock climbing – II. In snowy conditions, when used for descent, it can be quite difficult to find).

Effort: *From the north-east –* 800mH ascent to the Mittelaletsch Bivouac Hut (5-7 hrs), with a summit climb of 1200mH (5 hrs). *From the south-west –* hut climb 700mH, 8km (4 hrs), with a summit climb of 1700mH (7-8 hrs).

Dangers: On account of its situation amidst large glaciers and its isolated, wind-exposed position, the Aletschhorn is an unusually cold mountain, which makes the taking of warm and wind-proof clothing especially important. On the South-West Face, on the summit block, stone-fall is possible. On the glaciers there are the usual crevasse dangers. Otherwise both are objectively very safe climbs.

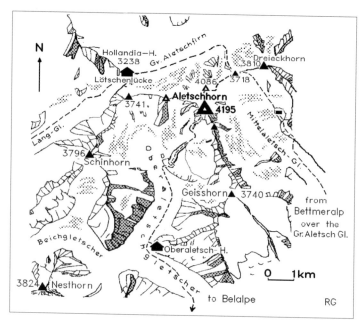

Pleasures: A magnificent, untouched mountain in a wild and isolated position.

Maps: LKS 1269 Aletsch Glacier and LKS 1249 Finsteraarhorn, also LKS 5004 Berner Oberland.

Travel: Along the Rhône valley by rail or car as far as Betten (830m; 5km south-west of Fiesch, 10km north-east of Brig, 3km from Morel). This is the valley station of the cableway to the *Bettmeralp* (1950m) a tourist resort on the shoulder of the ridge between the valley of the Grosser Aletsch Glacier and the Rhône valley.

For the South-West Face, by rail or car along the Rhône valley to Brig (684m), from there bus or car 9km up to the tourist village of *Blatten* (1322m).

Hut climbs: For the *North-East Ridge* start from Bettmeralp and climb down to the Bettmersee and follow a path to P.2292 on the ridge which runs south-west from the Eggishorn. A track leads in the direction of the Marjelensee on the West Face of the Bettmerhorn to almost below the Eggishorn. At P.2348.6, descend on the left to the Gross Aletsch Glacier and cross this (often laboriously) westwards to the junction with the Mittela-letsch Glacier. On this, first climb over moraine debris, then move onto the ice in the middle of the glacier. Above 2700m, avoid a more badly disrupted area on the right by a path on the eastern bank which leads to the *Mittelaletsch Bivouac Hut* at 3013m (SAC, 13 B, blankets, no kitchen, no wood).

South-West Face: from Blatten by cableway, or by car, to Täätsche 1750m, then in 1 hr on foot on zig-zag path, or by a little road to the cableway station on the Belalp (2094m). Head north-eastwards on broad path to Hotel Belalp (2130m). Behind it, descend a broad zig-zag track and then cross grassy slopes towards the head of the valley. Further on, climb to the moraine ramparts of the Oberaletsch Glacier descending from the left.

At about 2200m, the moraines are traversed. After that, ascend the dry glacier for about 3km to beyond and behind the spur on which the hut stands (easily seen, high above the polished rock). When beyond the confluence of the various glacier arms quit the glacier on a newly built path (red markings at start; pegs, wire ropes and chains) going up over the steep slabs 150mH to the very picturesque (but impractically placed for the Aletschorn ascent) *Oberaletsch Hut* (2640m; SAC Chassertal, 60 B, managed in summer, Tel. 028-27 17 67).

Summit climb by the North-East Ridge: From the Mittelaletsch Bivouac Hut, head north-west up over the crevassed slopes to the Aletschjoch (3629m). Turn to the west and follow the narrow corniced ridge of P.3718 (also reached from the north by the impressive Hasler Rib) to a broad snow slope. Climb this to the snow hump P.4086.3 which is crossed or turned on the south to gain the snow shoulder beyond. Finally climb a short steep slope, cross a bergschrund, finish up a snow and rock ridge to gain the summit.

Summit climb by the South-East Face: From the Oberaletsch Hut, descend the path back to the glacier and ascend it to about 2700m. After that, cross the marginal crevasse at a suitable place and, on a series of ledges and terraces (tracks; difficult to find in the dark), head obliquely right up to grass slopes. Climb the hollow between a rock rib (on the left) and a moraine (on the right) then go up a gully on the left to the crest granite spur with large blocks, and climb it to P.3382 at the upper end.

From here, take a right-left curve up the glacier (crevasses) to the foot of the rock spur descending from the summit. At first climb on the right of the spur, then move to the left to use a small snow-field which leads to the steeper gneiss rocks of the summit block. Take a line to the right of the edge, up a steep gully and straight on to a less steep snow-field which leads to the summit.

View: The summit provides a magnificent panorama. To the west is the Bietschhorn, and to the north and east are the other high Oberland summits. To the south, somewhat further away, are the giants of the Pennine Alps.

Adjacent peaks: On the North-East Ridge is the modest snow top of **P.4086**, on the West-North-West Ridge the scarcely more significant **P.4071** and, further west, the Kleines Aletschhorn (3755m). On the South-East Ridge is the prominent tower of P.3947.

Other worthwhile routes: *North Rib of P.3718 (Hasler Rib)* and *North-East Ridge* (AD+, pitch of III, mostly II and I, mixed, and snow to 50°, objectively safe; 700mH from the Grosser Aletschfirn to the ridge, then a further 500mH to the summit, 5-7 hrs from the Hollandia Hut).
South-East Ridge (AD−, II, mixed, 1600mH from Oberaletsch Hut 8 hrs).

Looking south-east to the Aletschhorn from the Gross-Grünhorn with the Grünegghorn in the foreground and the Grosser Aletschfirn beyond. In the distance are the high peaks of the Pennine Alps – Matterhorn, Weisshorn and Dent Blanche. The final part of the North-West Ridge goes up the large snow slopes below the summit, with the Hasler Rib just discernible as a sinuous edge leading diagonally up to the base of the upper slopes from the glacier basin.

West-North-West Ridge (AD+, III and II, 6-8 hrs from Obera-letsch Hut), most interesting as part of the large-scale *Lötschenlucke – Sattelhorn – Aletschhorn – Dreieckhorn Ridge traverse* (AD+, up to III; 11-15 hrs from Hollandia Hut to Konkordia Hut).

North Face (D/TD, thoroughbred ice climb, up to 50°, but lower part menaced by falling ice, 1100mH, 5-8 hrs).

Guidebook: Bernese Alps Central (The Alpine Club, London, 1979).

29

Jungfrau, 4158m

The name of this peak lends wings to the imagination, either as poetry or trivial jokes. For anyone who wants to read something original, Alphonse Daudet's delicious Alpine satire, *Tartarin on the Alps*, which has lost nothing of its freshness in the 100 years since it was written, is recommended. This third highest summit in the Bernese Alps is especially striking seen from the north. There the faces and snow slopes fall, a breathtaking 3000 metres, to the Lauterbrunnen valley. This magnificent mountain wall, together with its neighbours Mönch and Eiger, may be seen on clear days from the equally impressively frontages of the Swiss federal capital Berne. From the south the Jungfrau appears, by comparison, less magnificent, although even from there it still rises a good 1000 metres above the snow basin of the Grosser Aletsch Glacier.

The first ascent was made in 1811 by Johann Rudolf Meyer and Hieronymus Meyer with the chamois hunters Alois Volker and Joseph Bortis in a four-day expedition from the Lötschental. The rack-railway was built in 1912 up through the Eiger and Mönch to the Jungfraujoch. The outbreak of the First World War luckily prevented the planned continuation to the summit of the Jungfrau. The approach to the ordinary route can thus be considerably reduced by using the (at least) environmentally-preferable tunnel railway. To ascend this peak from the valley bottom entirely on foot is hard work.

Difficulties: PD+, climbing to II (mostly mixed) and snow or ice up to 40° and in part 50°. Late in the year, the bergschrund below the Rottalsattel can give problems.

Effort: The ascent from Jungfraujoch involves 850mH, and 150mH on the return (4 hrs from the Mönchsjoch Hut). The approach from south on foot from Fiesch gives 1100mH of ascent (3-4 hrs, avoidable by cableway) plus 750mH over a 10km stretch to the Konkordia Hut and from there summit climb of 1350mH over a further 7km stretch (5 hrs).

Dangers: A peak with a high accident rate. This is surely due to the easy access provided by the railway, which encourages less well prepared (and unacclimatized!) people to rash deeds. After fresh snow, the traverse to the Rottalsattel is often avalanche prone; also the cornices on the Rottalhorn can give trouble. More frequently the traverse from the Rottalsattel to the rocks is under-estimated. If everybody used the in-situ iron posts for belaying it would cut down the calls on the mountain rescue. On the glaciers there is constant crevasse danger and of course snow conditions deteriorate in the second half of the day. It is therefore strongly advised to spend a night in the hut making an early start, rather than a later one using the first morning train.

Pleasures: In good weather the descent is often spoiled by the crowds using the comfortable rail approach. Over-nighting in the Mönchsjoch Hut enables one – assuming some acclimatization – to start as early as one wishes. It also allows you to avoid the worst of the congestion.

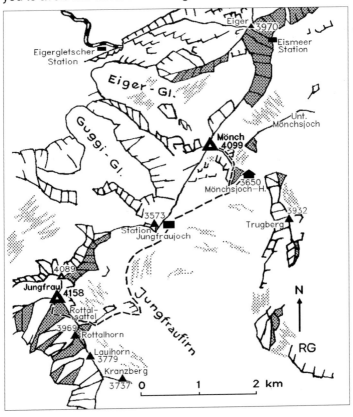

Maps: LKS 1249 Finsteraarhorn, also LKS 5004 Berner Oberland and LKS 264 Jungfrau.

Travel: By train from Berne via Interlaken to *Grindelwald* (1034m; elegant tourist resort, from there take the train to Jungfraujoch). By car via Interlaken to Grindelwald where there are the usual parking problems.

Hut climb: From the Jungfraujoch station (3475m) go through the Sphinxstollen tunnel and traverse under the South Face of the Mönch on a slightly ascending track to the Ober Mönchsjoch (1 hr) and then up east to the *Mönchsjoch Hut* (3660m, private, 125 B, managed in spring and summer, Tel. 036-71 34 72). For approach to the Konkordia Hut, see Grünhorn.

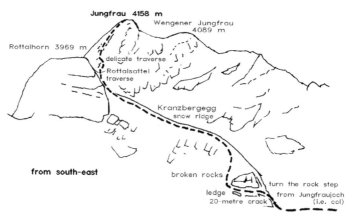

Summit climb: From the Mönchsjoch Hut, retrace the route to the Sphinxstollen. Then go south across the upper part of the Jungfraufirn, keeping below the base of the East Ridge of the Rottalhorn (Kranzbergegg) and climb up west and north to gain the ridge above P.3411.1.

Climb the broad scree-covered ridge (rain-gauge) to a steep step which is passed by a 20-metre crack leading to a narrow ledge (abseil point for descent). On the ledge under a high wall, go left (south) and then climb slabby rocks and snow straight up to the ridge. Continue on this on snow to about 3800m. Then traverse the North-East Face of the Rottalhorn high up, over the bergschrund, heading obliquely to the right, to the Rottalsattel (3885m). The traditional ascent direct from the Jungfrau Glacier to the Rottalsattel is, on account of large bergschrunds and steep ice, now invariably quite difficult.

From the Rottalsattel, make a tricky rising traverse left (north-westwards) on the steep slope to the rocks. It is worth belaying here – an accident blackspot. Continue up (numerous iron posts for belays) with technically easy climbing and then take the 35° snow slope leading to the summit rocks and highest point. The direct ascent from the Rottalsattel up over the 45° snow ridge is only advised in excellent conditions and even then it is more difficult than the described route.

View: To the west are the fierce ice faces at the upper end of the Lauterbrunnen valley. The Mönch is to the north-east. To the east and south are the big glaciers and the other high summits of the Bernese Oberland (Fiescherhorner, Gross-Grünhorn, Finster-aarhorn and the impressive and isolated Aletschhorn.

Adjacent peaks: The **Wengener Jungfrau (4089m)** marks the northern end of the summit ridge and is also the highest apex of the imposing North Face. 4000-metre purists will wish to reach this point as well (allow an extra 70 minutes). South of the Rottalsattel, the Rottalhorn (3969m) and beyond it the Lauihorn (3779m), as well as the Silberhorn (3695m), with its conspicuous North Face, are valued secondary goals.

Other worthwhile routes: *Innerer Rottalgrat or South-West Ridge* (AD, III and II, 1750 + 1400mH, 6 hrs from Rottal Hut).
Rotbrettgrat or North-West Ridge (D, if using fixed rope III, 1660 + 1500mH, 9 hrs from Silberhorn Hut).
Guggi Route (D+, A North Face traverse up hanging glaciers, serious, 480 + 1400mH, 8-10 hrs from the Guggi Hut).
North-East Ridge (D+, V and IV, 700mH, 8-9 hrs from Jungfraujoch).

Guidebook: Bernese Alps Central (The Alpine Club, 1979).

The Rottalhorn and the Jungfrau from the Mönch.

Mönch, 4099m

The Mönch lies so close to the Jungfraujoch that the ascent by the ordinary route, just like that of the Breithorn and Allalinhorn, has received undue emphasis; for in doing so one gets to know merely the uppermost few hundred metres of the mountain. Yet that should not be taken lightly, especially if one is unfit. Under-estimating the task can lead to over-straining and failure as the technical difficulties of the climb are far from negligible and when icy are often increased. The first ascent was made in August 1857 by the well-known Grindelwald guide Christian Almer and Ulrich and Christian Kaufmann with the Viennese Siegismund Porges. The daring coup of the first ascent of the popular Nollen on the north-west flank fell to the Berne climber Edmund von Fellenberg with the guides Christian Michel and Peter Egger as far back as 1866. This was long before the development of adequate ice equipment and proved a truly hair-raising undertaking (a 10-metre ladder taken as an aid proved useless).

Difficulties: PD. Rock climbing to II, mixed, and snow or ice to 45°.
Effort: To summit from Mönchsjoch Hut 500mH (2-3 hrs).
Dangers: Under-estimating the demands of the mountain and trying to 'bag' it without adequate acclimatization, practice and experience. On bare ice, belaying with ice screws is recommended. Look out for cornices on the very narrow summit ridge! Even without cornices it is very precarious and exposed. It is best to keep just below the crest on the south side if possible.
Pleasures: A peak for which a brief weather improvement suffices, with a short, but very attractive climb.

Maps, sketches, travel and hut climb: See Jungfrau.
Summit climb: From the Oberes Mönchsjoch, traverse south-westwards for 400m to the foot of the South Spur (P.3651; or reach the same point direct from the Sphinxstollen of the Jungfrau railway, climbing north-eastwards. On the spur, climb debris then slabs, at first on limestone then further up more steeply on reddish gneiss, past the rain-gauge to P.3887. Here the South Spur joins the East-South-East Ridge.

Continue along an almost horizontal snow or rock ridge (beware of cornices) to a steeper, rocky piece of ridge. Climb its edge, awkward when icy, to a further snow ridge. Over this, partly broken by rock steps, to a steeper ice passage. This leads to the junction (fore-summit) with the branch of the ridge ascending from the north-east. Keep on the south side of the narrow summit ridge, taking care to avoid cornices, to gain the highest point on the spacious summit.

View: The view is dominated by the contrast between the steep drop to the north and the grassy foothills, and the extensive glaciers and icy summits to the south. To the north-east the Eiger is situated immediately ahead, to the east the Schreckhorn group, to the south-east the Fiescherhornen, the Finsteraarhorn and Gross-Grünhorn. Opposite, to the west, lies the Jungfrau, to the south-west, somewhat more distant, the icy pyramid of the Aletschhorn.

Adjacent peaks: The fore-summit (c.4065m) is only a suggestion.

Other worthwhile routes: *South-West Ridge* (AD–, direct from the Jungfraujoch, III and II, 650mH, 3-4 hrs).
North-East Face (D, snow or ice to 57°, mostly 45°, 250mH, 3 hrs from starting climb).
North-West Spur or Nollen (D, ice to 65°, from the Guggi Hut 480 + 1300mH, 7 hrs).
North Face Rib or Lauper Route (D+/TD, rock to V– and snow or ice to 60+; 1300mH, 10-12 hrs from the Guggi Hut; large-scale but objectively not very dangerous).
Guidebook: Bernese Alps East (The Alpine Club, 1979).

Mönch from south-west with the route following the right skyline.

Gross-Fiescherhorn, 4049m

Seen from Grindelwald, where its impact vies with that of the Eiger, this is a wild and menacing wall. When viewed from the Ewigschneefeld it is less spectacular but still attractive as a considerable ridge crest. The first ascent in 1862 fell to the Grindelwald guides Christian Almer and Ulrich Kaufmann with A.W. Moore (later known for the first ascent of the Brenva Face of Mont Blanc) and H.B. George.

Difficulties: PD+. A glacier route with climbing to II and I.
Effort: From the Mönchsjoch Hut the summit climb involves 750mH, with a reascent of 350mH when returning: from the Konkordia Hut it is 1350mH; from Finsteraarhorn Hut 1000mH.
Dangers: On the glaciers there are the customary crevasse hazards. On parts of the ascent from the Konkordia Hut there is danger of falling ice, likewise on the ascent from the Finsteraarhorn Hut. On the final slope to the Fiechersattel, there is stone-fall danger when following other parties.
Pleasures: A wonderful vantage point in the centre of the wildest part of the Oberland. Ski mountaineers also get their money's worth here: Easter and Whitsun often producing alarming crowds of people.

Maps, sketches, travel and hut climb: See Jungfrau, Grünhorn and Finsteraarhorn.
Summit climb: *From the Mönchsjoch Hut* head eastwards and then south-eastwards down across the Ewigschneefeld to 3300m. (This part is also reached from Konkordia by an ascent up the Ewigschneefeld ice-fall taking a line to the south of the main fall. This is less crevassed but more menaced by falling ice than the Mönchsjoch Hut approach.) Now ascend on the left (north) of the rock rib descending from P.3981 of the Hinter-Fiescherhorn to P.3415 and continue keeping left, up under the West Face of the Hinter-Fiescherhorn. On the final section the best line is left (north-west) of the saddle fall line, over the often big bergschrund and then, keeping right, over the steep and often icy slope to brittle slate rocks. These lead to the Fiechersattel (3923m, 3-4 hrs from the Mönchsjoch Hut). The final section can be avoided by traversing to P.3711 on the rock rib on the left of the crevassed slopes and following this to the summit.

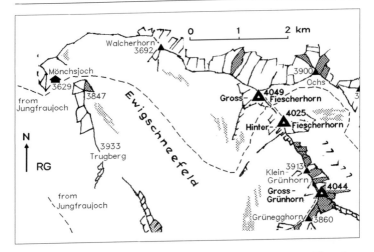

From the Finsteraarhorn Hut ascend the upper Fiescher Glacier as far as west of point P.3443.8. Beyond this, head up the ice-fall, keeping right, for about 120mH. This is a steep slope with often hungry crevasses and dangers of falling ice. Then work round to the left, towards Ochs, on the flatter, upper slopes of the glacier to about 3700m, then head west up to the Fiechersattel (4-5 hrs from Finsteraarhorn Hut; see Grünhorn and Lauteraarhorn sketches).

From the Fiechersattel (now joint route), continue on the South-East Ridge to a slabby rock tower. Climb over this (III−) or turn it on the right on steep snow or ice. After that, continue up the ridge on firm gneiss to the summit (4-5 hrs from the Mönchsjoch Hut, 5-6 hrs from the Finsteraarhorn Hut, 6-7 hrs from the Konkordia Hut).

View: To the south-east is the Hinter-Fiescherhorn and to the right, behind that, the more rugged Gross-Grünhorn, to the east is the Finsteraarhorn, to the north-east behind the Ochs are the Schreckhorn and the Lauteraarhorn, to the west the Mönch and northwards, near it, the Eiger. To the north is a majestic view down the imposing Fiescherwand.

Adjacent peaks: 4000m top collectors will wish to bag the neighbouring Hinter-Fiescherhorn but the ascent of over 100m from the intervening col rather prohibits that. The Ochs (also known as Klein-Fiescherhorn, 3900m) to the east-north-east, is a feasible addition if based at the

Finsteraarhorn Hut. The climb to this finishes along an airy, narrow, corniced ridge.

Other worthwhile routes: *North-West Ridge* (AD, III, mixed, and ice to 50+, 4km long ridge from the Unteren Mönchsjoch, often luxuriantly corniced, 4-5 hrs from the Mönchsjoch Hut. *North Rib to P.3804* (TD+, IV and III, mixed and serious. Approached over a ragged glacier, then an ascent of 1000mH from start of climb, 10 hrs).
North Face Direct (ED, IV mixed, ice to 65°, 1300mH, one of the hardest ice faces in the Alps).

Guidebook: Bernese Alps East (The Alpine Club, 1979).

Hinter-Fiescherhorn, 4025m

The southern neighbour of the Gross-Fiescherhorn is climbed (PD) from the Fiechersattel in about an hour. Usually one keeps to the east of the ridge on the gently inclined slopes left of the deep potholes, and only on the final part going directly on the snow ridge. From the Ewigschneefeld approach one can also climb the inclined rock rib south of the Gross-Fiesherhorn route (traverse the big rock tower on the left, II) to the prominent rocky South Ridge Summit P.3981 and from there traverse the summit (PD). For further information, see Gross-Fiescherhorn.

Gross-Fiescherhorn and Hinter-Fiescherhorn (behind it, the Finsteraarhorn).

Gross-Grünhorn, 4044m

A beautifully formed peak with stylish rock ridges high above wild glaciers. The summit block consists of firm amphibolite. Its situation, far from mountain railways and motor passes, still guarantees the ascent a really alpine character.

At the Konkordia Hut, the glacier shrinkage of the last 140 years is especially noticeable. At the time of the glacier high point in 1850, the rock shoulders, on which the huts were erected, lay more or less at the same height as the upper surface of the Grosser Aletsch Glacier. Yet today, even after a decline in height of some 100m, the thickness of the ice at the Konkordiaplatz, by seismic measurements, still amounts to about 900 metres.

The first ascent of this peak was made in 1885 by the Berne climber Edmund von Fellenberg with his guides Peter Egger, Peter Michel and Peter Innit from the Ewigschneefeld.

Difficulties: PD+. On approach to the Grünegghorn, snow to 40° and easy climbing (pitches of I). On the summit ridge there are exposed sections of III– and II, which can be quite difficult when icy.

Effort: The hut climb from the cableway station above Fiesch is 750mH and 12km, 5 hrs. If the cableway is shunned, there is an additional 1100mH and 4km, 3-4 hrs. Alternatively, approach from the Jungfraujoch to the Konkordiaplatz (2-3 hrs). From the hut, the summit climb is 1400mH.

Dangers: There are some crevasses on the Grüneggfirn otherwise, in good conditions, this is an objectively safe climb.

Pleasures: The peak offers everything that an alpinist treasures – remoteness, history, excellent views, good climbing.

Maps: LKS 1249 Finsteraarhorn, for approach from south LKS 1269 Gr.Aletsch Gletscher or LKS 5004 Berner Oberland.

Travel: By rail or car through the Rhône valley to *Fiesch* (1049m; not too large a tourist resort with attractive old houses in the town centre, cableway to Eggishorn). For approach from Jungfraujoch, see Jungfrau.

Hut climbs: From the middle station of the Eggishorn cableway (Chuebodenstafel, 2221m), go north-east on a broad track along the slope. Then climb round a ridge

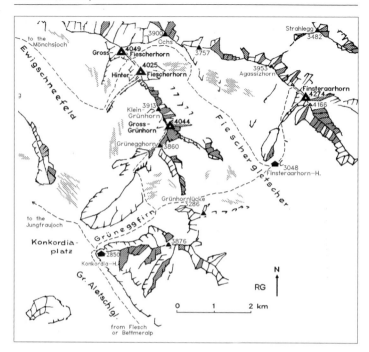

(P.2386, view of Fiescher Glacier) and descend to the west across the Marjelenalpe to the picturesque Marjelensee, which is dammed in by the ice of the Grosser Aletsch Glacier. Move onto the dry (in summer) glacier, first of all going through crevasse zones, then on clearer terrain, gradually ascending the eastern part of this impressive and extensive ice stream heading north, then north-north-west. In mist, the debris ramparts of the central moraines make route-finding easier. After several kilometres, adher closely to the eastern glacier bank (often transverse crevasses full of snow), pass under the huts and then, from the west, reach the beginning of the iron ladders and stairs screwed to the almost vertical polished rock. Ascend 100mH to the *Konkordia Hut* (2850m; SAC Grindelwald; 130 B, managed in spring and summer, Tel. 036-55 13 94).

Approach from Jungfraujoch: From the Jungfraujoch station, through the Sphinxstollen to the Jungfraufirn. Descend this keeping close to the eastern (left) edge under the slopes of the Trugberg and then below the ice-falls of the Ewigschneefeld coming in from the east, to the glacier morass of the Konkordiaplatz to arrive at the iron ladders from the north.

Summit climb by the South-West Ridge: From the Konkordia Hut descend the ladders and ascend eastwards over the Gruneggfirn to about 3000m. Keeping close to the northern edge of the glacier, ascend more steeply for about 400mH. Then turn left (west) over snow slopes and a short steep gully to the south-west pointing snow slope of the Grünegghorn. Follow this to the fore-summit (3787m). Continue along an exposed rocky ridge with a final rise, keeping a respectful distance from the occasional cornices on the right, to reach the summit of the Grünegghorn (3860m, 3-4 hrs from the Konkordia Hut).

Descend the steep rock ridge to the saddle beyond (c.3800m) This point can be reached from the Ewigschneefeld by the serious and complicated glacier route used on the first ascent. This can be time-consuming and is only advantageous in spring snow conditions.

From the saddle continue along the rocky South-West Ridge, sometimes using the slope to the left, to the summit of the Gross-Grünhorn.

View: To the west there is an impressive view of the source of the longest Alpine glacier with the icy Aletschhorn and the Jungfrau above it. The impressively towering Finsteraarhorn dominates the eastern view. To the north are the Fiescherhorner, the Eiger and the Mönch.

Adjacent peaks: The Grünegghorn (3860m), immediately to the south-west, is traversed on the ordinary route. The Klein-Grünhorn (3913m), a similar distance away to the north-west, is more easily climbed from the Ewigschneefeld over the Kleine Grünhornlucke and the North-North-West Ridge (II) (5 hrs from the Konkordia Hut).

Other worthwhile routes: *North-North-West Ridge* from the Klein-Grünhorn (D, IV and III, 3-4 hrs from summit to summit). *South-East Ridge and South-East Face* (AD+, III, mixed, from the Finsteraarhorn Hut 1000mH, 4-6 hrs). *East Spur* (TD–, V–, mixed; worthwhile rock-climbing, 650mH of rock, 7-9 hrs from foot of face).

Guidebook: Bernese Alps East (The Alpine Club, 1979).

These mountains between Grimsel and the Fiescher Glaciers and Eismeer are especially wild and remote and have a particularly grand and dominant character. Even on repeat ascents they always retain their interest.

Schreckhorn, 4078m

The most rugged and hardest of the Bernese 4000ers is largely a rock peak. Despite its considerable difficulty, it was first climbed as early as in 1861 by Leslie Stephen with the guides Christian and Peter Michel and Ulrich Kaufmann. Today's customary ordinary route was discovered in 1907 by J.H. Wicks, E.H.F. Bradby and C. Wilson. The enormous approaches from all quarters maintains the Schreckhorn as one of the most exacting peaks in the Alps.

Difficulties: AD+. Rock-climbing III and II, mixed. However, after new snow it dries off quickly at the critical places. Nevertheless, the traverse from the glacier to the rock can present problems in some years. This climb is particularly tiring because of the sustained nature of the difficulties, both on the ascent and descent.

Effort: Hut climb 1570mH (5-6 hrs; with use of cableway 1160mH, 4-5 hrs), summit climb 1558mH (of which 600mH is on the summit tower (7-8 hrs).

Dangers: In contrast to the route used by the first ascent party, by the Schreckhorn Couloir and the Schrecksattel, the customary ascent today up the South-West Ridge is objectively less dangerous. However, it should not be under-estimated; here too crevasses lie in wait on the glacier and the ramp is exposed to stone-fall.

Pleasures: Varied climbing on sound gneiss, in impressive position.

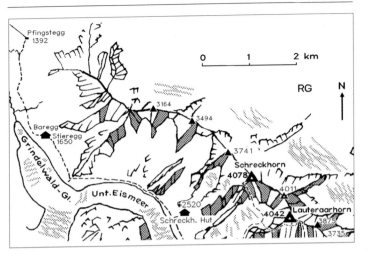

Maps: LKS 1229 Grindelwald, also LKS 5004 Berner Oberland. See also Lauteraarhorn sketch, photograph and topo.

Travel: To Grindelwald, see Jungfrau.

Hut climb: Take the Pfingstegg cableway to 1392m and then traverse south-west to join the hut path at P.1386. (Or reach the same point, sportingly on foot, starting at the Lutschinen Bridge and taking a marked track up to the hamlet of Uf der Halten and thence south of the Toldislouwina, climbing the zig-zag path through the wood.)

Continue southwards on a shelf above sections of steep rock to Begg and somewhat downwards to Gasthaus Stieregg (1650m accommodation, 2-3 hrs from Grindelwald). Now ascend east over grass and moraines and continue south to the spur of the Banisegg. After that, eastwards above the Unteren Eismeer Glacier to the steep rocks of Rots Gufer. Traverse across and climb these on constructed paths (ropes, pegs, aluminium ladders) and cross some streams. Then, before reaching the remains of the old Schwarzegg Hut, work left (east) over a moraine to the new *Schreckhorn Hut* (2520m, SAC Basle, 90 B, managed in summer, Tel. 036-55 10 25).

Summit climb: From the hut, descend to the Obers Eismeer and continue along the old hut path to the remains of the

Strahlegg Hut (destroyed by avalanches). Ascend north-eastwards up the snow and debris-filled Gaagg valley to about 2950m, then move left to the notch above P.2844 on the brittle rock rib of the 'Gaagg'. Climb this, in part on groaning blocks, to reach a snow-field (3150m).

Now, after a short ascent to the left over snow, traverse to the upper part of the Schreckfirn and across in an arc to the foot of the conspicious South Face Couloir bisecting the red rocks of the South Face (3 hrs). The direct ascent to here up the Lower Schreck Couloir is shorter but objectively dangerous.

Cross the bergschrund on the left of the couloir (late in the year this is often exciting) and work up and then across left to the bottom left edge of a ramp which slants up to the left. Ascend the rocky edge of the big, mostly snow-filled, ramp (III in good conditions, but when iced it is more pleasant to climb the snow of the ramp) to a shoulder of the South-West Ridge (c.3800m). Climb the ridge keeping close to the steep and narrowing knife-edge (III) and continue until a steep step bars the way. Climb this direct (IV) or on the left side (III) and regain the ridge which is followed steeply, with fine climbing (III) to a snow ridge which leads (cornice possible) on to the summit.

View: Uniformly impressive. To the north lies Grindelwald dominated by the limestone summit of the Wetterhorn and to the east is the Lauteraar Glacier. To the south, beyond the nearby Lauteraarhorn is the majestic Finsteraarhorn, with the Fiescherhorner and the Grünhorn to its right. To the west, above the ice-falls of the Eismeer, are the Mönch and Eiger and behind them the tip of the Jungfrau.

Descent: From the fore-summit on the South-West Ridge make three 40m abseils on the edge or climb down 20m on the west side and then use a ledge to get back to the edge, on which one can then climb down further to the shoulder at the beginning of the steep ramp (if the snow is rotten late in the day, then it is better to climb down the edge of the ramp).

Other worthwhile routes: *North-West Ridge or Andersongrat* (D, III, mixed, 1750mH, 8 hrs from the Gleckstein Hut to the summit).

South Pillar (TD–, V– and IV, enjoyable climbing for experts, from foot of face 600mH, 5-6 hrs).

Guidebook: Bernese Alps East (The Alpine Club, 1979).

Lauteraarhorn, 4042m

This southern high peak of the 10km Schreckhorn crest stands in every respect way behind the valley of the Grindelwald Glacier, way behind the valley of the Lauteraar Glacier, way behind in height, and, consequently, also way behind on the lists of desirable summits.

Up to 1976, an ascent still meant a voluntary bivouac had to be planned, but it should be remembered that in the days of the pioneers, this was the norm everywhere. The first to climb the peak in 1842, the geologist Arnold Escher from Linth and the glaciologists Eduard Desor and Christian Girard, made their bivouac in an uncomfortable situation by a gigantic block on the central moraine of the Unteraar Glacier.

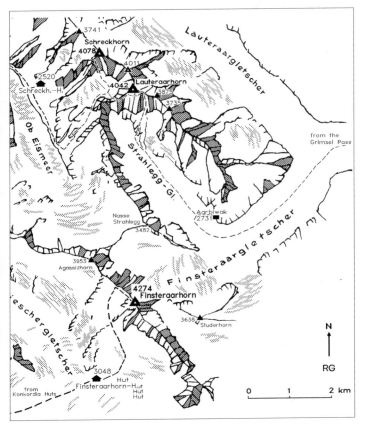

From there they explored the glaciers in the vicinity, under the climbing leadership of the local men Melchior Bannholzer and Jakob Leuthold, and then climbed the Lauteraarhorn by mistake – the Schreckhorn having been their real goal.

Since the building of the Aar Bivouac Hut, the ascent can be preceeded by a comfortable night's sleep. This allows the most convenient final climb but the price is a very long approach up the eastern Oberland glaciers. If, despite many protests, the brutal project of enlarging the Grimsel Reservoir (Super-Grimsel) should become a reality, despite all the protests, the initial part of this approach march will become considerably less convenient and enjoyable than today.

Difficulties: AD+. By the South Face Couloir with snow or ice to 40°, and thence by the South-East Ridge with rock-climbing of II, mixed. The couloir can be difficult to pinpoint in the dark.

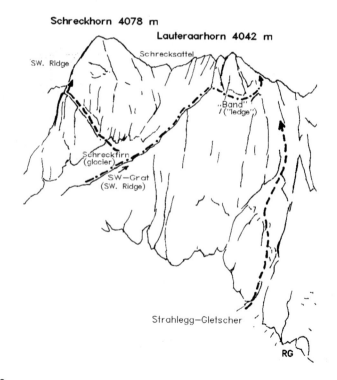

The Shreckhorn and Lauteraarhorn from the south-west.

Effort: The climb to bivouac hut involves 900mH and 19km of walking (7 hrs), the summit climb is 1300mH (5-6 hrs), of which 900mH is in the couloir and on the ridge. The summit ascent from the Schreckhorn Hut is 1550mH, 7-8 hrs, but with a slightly shorter approach.

47

Dangers: The South Face Couloir can be considerably threatened by ridge cornices. This is true even when one keeps to the flanking rocks. In the interests of safety, the timing must allow a descent of the couloir before the snow has softened. If the snow is soft in the morning, one should not start at all. The ascent 'Uber das Band' (Over the Ledge) is delicate.

Pleasures: One of the most remote areas of the Alps.

Maps: LKS 1229 Grindelwald, LKS 1249 Finsteraarhorn, LKS 1250 Ulrichen, also LKS 5004 Berner Oberland.

Travel: By rail from the north via Berne and Interlaken to Meiringen, from the east via Chur and the Furka tunnel, from the south-west through the Rhône valley via Brig to Oberwald. From Meiringen and Oberwald, by bus to *Grimsel Stausee* [reservoir] and the Staumauer Grimselhospiz (1980m, beds for climbers).

Hut Climb: From the car-park terrace of the hospice, take the concrete steps into the basement and cross the dam wall to the north bank of the reservoir. There, climb steps and go through a tunnel, then under the artificial but very considerable waterfall of a supply tunnel. Continue along pretty flagged paths past magnificent Arolla pines. These, together with the first pitches of the wonderful El Dorado slabs further up the valley, would be drowned if the Super-Grimsel was allowed. After the present (and hopefully the future) end of the reservoir, move over moraines to the Unteraar Glacier and follow the markings along a central moraine. Further on, the markings point to a big block on the northern bank, from whence a path on the side moraine leads to the Lauteraar Hut (2392m, SAC Zofingen, 50 B, managed in summer from time to time, Tel. 036-73 11 10; 4-5 hrs from Grimselhospiz; ladder path to the Unteraar Glacier).

After regaining the glacier, stay on the central moraine and subsequently go left to the Finsteraarhorn Glacier coming in from the south-west. Up this, along the central moraine, to the junction of the Strahlegg Glacier coming from the north-west. Now follow marker poles, staying on the level glacier, passing a crevasse zone on the east side, until as far as the fall line of the bivouac hut and only then (following the coloured markings) go across to the *Aar Bivouac Hut* (2731m; SAC Pilatus, 17 B, blankets, no cooking equipment).

Summit climb by South Face Couloir and South-East Ridge: from the Aar Bivouac, climb up over the Strahlegg Glacier, passing the ice of the steep tributary glacier embedded in the slope on the right, until below the mouth of the prominent couloir. The best line starts left of this, climbing blocks to a snow shoulder (c.3250m). Up the ridge to the left (west) bordering rib of the couloir. Climb this (I) to a small snow saddle somewhat west of the prominent tower of P.3915. In good conditions this can be reached more pleasantly but with more objective danger by just climbing the couloir. From the snow saddle go directly up the slabby gneiss ridge (II) enjoyably to the summit.

West-South-West Ridge with the traverse to the South-East Ridge: From the Schreckhorn Hut take the Schreckhorn approach up to 3150m on the snow-field above the Gaagg. Move right over snow, or the rocks left of that (below P.3428) to gain the Strahlegg Pass (3345m). From here continue up the somewhat brittle ridge to a saddle. Then, keeping on the right, turn a steep rise (in part III– and II) to gain a big shoulder (c.3750m). From here follow a snow ridge to the foot of the difficult summit wall. To avoid this involves a long traverse across the South Face taking a not very obvious ledge system, ascending and descending (in parts delicate, pitches of II) crossing rock ribs and gullies before finally using a rubbish chute to gain the South-East Ridge and thence to the summit (6-7 hrs from the Schreckhorn Hut).

View: Similar to that from the Schreckhorn, with particularly interesting views of the Finsteraarhorn towering up to the south-west.

Adjacent peaks: The fairly prominent **North-West Ridge summit P.4011** can only to be reached by a long ridge climb (up to IV).

Other worthwhile routes: *North-West Ridge from the Schreckhorn* (D, pitches of IV, in part easier gives a classic long ridge climb, 5-6 hrs from summit to summit).

West-South-West Ridge Direct (TD, V and IV, splendid crack climbing on the summit wall provides an excellent direct finish to the above described ridge route, 8-9 hrs from the Schreckhorn Hut).

East Rib of the North-West Ridge of P.4011 (D, IV, 1000mH from the foot of the rib, 1600mH, 10-12 hrs from the Lauteraar Hut).

Guidebook: Bernese Alps East (The Alpine Club, 1979).

Finsteraarhorn, 4273m

The highest summit in the Bernese Alps, towering above all the surrounding peaks provides a selection of elegant lines of ascent. Likewise, the glacier scenery of its surroundings is amongst the most imposing in the Alps. The Fiescherhorn Glacier below, forced into a narrow valley, exceeds, in terms of length, even the great ice streams of Mont Blanc and Monte Rosa. Despite the length of its approaches this regal mountain is very popular. However, this happens mainly in the spring when skis allow a more rapid approach. At this time the hut is frequently overcrowded during spells of good weather. In summer the endless trudging along the wide glacier basins deters all but the most dedicated alpinists.

The mountain was first climbed in 1812 from the south-east. As the paying clients, Rudolf Meyer and Kaspar Huber remained behind on a fore-summit and only the three guides Alois Volker, Joseph Bortis and Arnold Abbuhl went on further, their report of reaching the highest point was later disputed. With certainty the summit was reached in 1829 – via today's ordinary route – by the guides Jakob Leuthold and Johann Wahren, while the geologist and glaciologist Franz Joseph Hugi remained behind a little below the summit (nevertheless to be immortalized in the naming of the Hugisattel). A particularly impressive early ascent was that of the classy East-North-East-Spur in 1904 by the guide Fritz Amatter and the Swiss Gustav Hasler. The upper part of this route, menaced by stone-fall, was straightened in 1930 and 1967.

Difficulties: PD. To Hugisattel a glacier climb with snow to 35°. On the North-West Ridge of the summit block there is exposed climbing to II on firm gneiss (often icy, then distinctly harder).

Effort: Hut climb from Jungfraujoch via Konkordiaplatz, 1000mH descent, 500mH ascent, 13km (5 hrs); from Konkordia Hut 500mH ascent and 200mH of descent (3-4 hrs); plus from the cableway above Fiesch also 750mH and 123km; from Fiesch

The Finsteraarhorn from the Hinter-Fiescherhorn.

via the Fiescher Glacier 2100mH (8-10 hrs); from the Grimselsee via Oberaarjoch and Gemslücke, altogether 1500mH ascent, 7-9 hrs. Summit climb 1300mH (4-5 hrs).

Dangers: On the glacier there are occasionally awkward crevasses, and cornices on the summit ridge. Otherwise, objectively, a very safe climb.

Pleasures: The climb is particularly fine on the summit block, as a comprehensive panorama gradually unfolds and broadens.

Maps: LKS 1249 Finsteraarhorn, also LKS 5004 Berner Oberland. See also Grünhorn and Lauteraarhorn sketches.

Travel: By rail or car to *Grindelwald* (see Jungfrau) or Fiesch (see Gross-Grünhorn).

Hut climbs: To the Konkordiaplatz, see Gross-Grünhorn. On the Gruneggfirn, ascend eastwards through the snow troughs to the Grünhornlucke and on the other side go down in the glacier trough (crevasses) to the Fiescher Glacier. After crossing it, there is a short ascent to the *Finsteraarhorn Hut* which lies below P.3231 on the east bank (3048m; 115 B, managed in spring and periodically in summer, Tel. 036-55 29 55).

Summit climb by the South-West Face and the North-West Ridge: From the hut follow a path to the north-east over the debris ridge (or left of that on snow) to the saddle by P.3231. Continue to the north over the glacier (crevasses) and on the right of a rock spur through a trough to the 'Frühstücksplatz' (breakfast place) on P.3616 of the South-West Ridge.

Continue northwards on the glacier on the left of the South-West Ridge crossing bergschrunds higher to reach

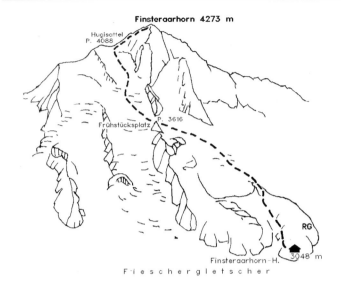

the Hugisattel (by P.4088, 4094 on Sheet 5004). Follow the North-West Ridge, first on the west side and then on the ridge proper (II) to the summit. (Note: If the North-West Ridge is crowded, the direct ascent from P.3616 up the South-West Ridge offers an only slightly more difficult alternative, PD+).

View: To the north-east to the Lauteraarhorn and Schreckhorn, with their glaciers flowing towards the Grimsel Pass, to the east the Urner Alps, to the south-west, behind the crest of the Wannenhorn, the Pennine Alps, and to the west is the Gross-Grünhorn, with its rugged East Face especially impressive.

Adjacent peaks: The **North-West Ridge summit P.4088** by the Hugisattel is not especially prominent, somewhat more distinct is the **South-East fore-summit P.4166.**

Other worthwhile routes: *South-East Ridge* (AD, III, mixed, and snow to 50°, a classic ridge, 2.5km long, 1100mH, 10-12 hrs from the Gemslücke to the summit).

East-North-East Spur (D+ to TD, long passages IV+, elegant classic climbing on good gneiss – the 'Walker Spur' of the Bernese Alps, 850mH of rock, 8-10 hrs from start of climb).

Guidebook: Bernese Alps East (The Alpine Club, 1979).

Pennine Alps (Valais or Wallis)

The Pennine Alps constitute the backbone of the Alps. This enormous massif includes more than half the 4000ers of this whole gigantic fold mountain system. From the frontier crest, along which most of the highest peaks are to be found, huge, deeply entrenched valleys run northwards to the Rhône valley which in the Ice Age was also fed by the glaciers of the Bernese Oberland to the north. These valleys are, because of their situation to leeward of the high mountains, extraordinarily dry, so that traditional Alpine husbandry has, for many centuries, relied on artificial irrigation of the pastures. From the permanently flowing glacier streams, the water is led along the slopes to the meadows in laboriously constructed trenches and canal systems and there distributed via branching ditches.

If the more recent tourist developments in the valley villages have robbed the Valais district of its traditional appearance, there are still, as witness to the old peasant culture, many groups of the typical wooden houses and granaries to be found, which to the visitors are as photogenic as the lofty, glittering snow mountain giants. One can really appreciate again the normal, mild world down below, when, worn-out and brutalised by exposure to the savage alps, one returns to the warm green of the valleys.

The description of the mountains starts with the mountain crests lying between the valleys, in each case from north to south, after that the frontier crest from east to west is described.

Old Valais peasant houses.

53

This side crest has two different faces. The western Saastal is thoroughly developed with roads and cableways. The eastern side on the other hand is only accessible by car as far as Simplon. Otherwise access is by foot up long and tiring valleys which conspire to use up all reserves of energy, before the bases of the mountains are reached.

Lagginhorn, 4010m

The most north-easterly and lowest 4000er of the Pennine Alps, at least as long as the plans to promote the northern neighbouring Fletschhorn from its 3993 metres (through building measures) to a 4000er are not realized. The Lagginhorn reaches the magic line without such assistance, only by ten metres it is true, but with elegance. The summit soars small and airy over deep abysses. Its first ascent was made in 1856 by the Saas pastor Johann Joseph Imseng and his servant Friedrich Joseph Andenmatten, as well as seven other companions. These included four Englishmen, their presence a harbinger of the development of the tourist industry. The classic ascent route was then, as now, by the rocky West Ridge. Indeed the Lagginhorn is, in summer, mostly a very rocky mountain, with snow-fields and glaciers mere arabesques on the extensive gneiss faces.

Difficulties: PD. Easy rock-climbing with a pitch of II, otherwise I and scrambling on good gneiss.
Effort: 1280mH ascent, 4-5 hrs from the Weissmies Hut; 960mH, 3-4 hrs from the cableway station at Hohsaas.
Dangers: Objectively a very safe climb. The crevasses on the small Lagginhorn Glacier are avoidable by an ascent from the base of the West Ridge. In the upper part there may be stone-fall danger from climbing parties above.
Pleasures: Some entertaining rock-climbing in the middle part of the ridge. An open panorama from summit. In reliable weather and on dry rock, a later departure is possible as the ascent can be made without using the snow slope.

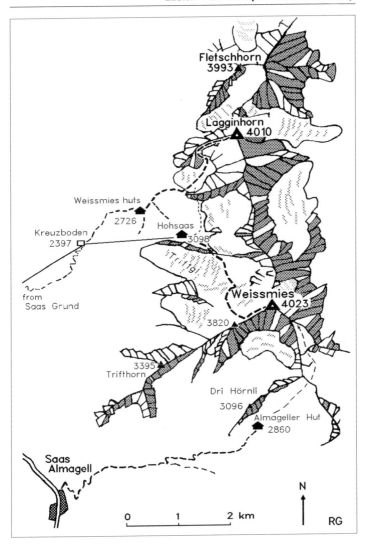

Maps: LKS 1309 Simplon, LKS 5006 Matterhorn-Mischabel.

Travel and Hut climbs: See Weissmies.

Summit route by the West Ridge: From the Weissmies Huts head north-east over grassy ridges and a ramp to the glacier stream. Ascend the path on the left (north) of this on moraine ridges (with steep, short bends near the top)

55

to the beginning of the prominent ridge which divides the Hohlaub Glacier (south) from the Lagginhorn Glacier (north). Ascend on the left over moraine debris and snow, pass south of the tongue of the Lagginhorn Glacier and then go up over the glacier to its northern upper end. From there move left (west) to a big block terrace (2 hrs). To reach this point from the *Hohsaas* cableway station: head north-east, descending somewhat to the Hohlaub Glacier. Traverse under the tongue, following little cairns, over debris and slabs (delicate when icy!) to the other side of the glacier. There, ascend obliquely left over a slabby ramp (little cairns, pitches of II), then traverse and finally climb again to the ridge between Hohlaub Glacier and Lagginhorn Glacier. Move to the other side until almost level with the Lagginhorn Glacier and continue as previously described to the block terrace (1 hr).

From the block terrace head north-eastwards, following the picturesque cairns to the ridge (which can also be climbed direct, without reference to the glaciers). Follow the crampon scratches and path on the southern flank (various possibilities) moving steadily upwards in the direction of the mountain. Finally go directly along the crest, with a touch of exposure on the view down to the Fletschhorn Glacier. Continue (pitch of II on a slab) to the notch before the poorly defined upper part of the ridge. Climb debris and rock. Avoid the snow-field by traversing right as low as possible and thence go up to the summit block. Continue, keeping near the edge on the right to finally make a surprisingly airy finish to gain the highest point.

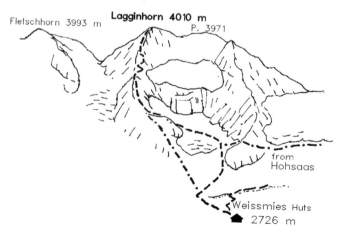

Fletschhorn 3993 m   **Lagginhorn 4010 m**   P. 3971

from Hohsaas

Weissmies Huts 2726 m

Weissmies from the Lagginhorn.

View: To the south the nearby Weissmies with its icy North-West Face dominates. On the far side of the Saas valley is the mighty crest from Monte Rosa to the Nadelgrat. To the north, behind the nearby Fletschhorn, are the Bernese Alps, and to the east the Simplon and the expanses of the Engadine as well as, in the distance, the Bernina.

Adjacent peaks: South Summit (3971m) is a not very prominent elevation on the South Ridge.

Other worthwhile routes: *South Ridge* (AD, III and II, mixed, brittle to start with), via the Lagginjoch, 5 hrs from Hohsaas. *North Ridge* (AD, III and II, mixed, in part corniced), 2-3 hrs from the Fletschhorn, via the Fletschhornjoch. *East Spur* (AD+, III, brittle, 1700mH, 6-7 hrs from the Laggin Bivouac Hut.)

Guidebooks: Pennine Alps East (The Alpine Club, 1975).

Weissmies, 4023m

This is the highest mountain in the north-eastern Pennine Alps, east of the Saas valley, and is at the same time the most beautiful. Its ice-armoured North-West Face contrasts strongly with the steep, mostly bare gneiss face of the south side over which mighty summit ridge cornices project.

Correspondingly different are its ordinary routes. The older and easier (not assisted by the cableway) takes the South-East Ridge. The mountain was first climbed by this way in 1856 by Peter Joseph Zurbriggen and Jakob Christian Heuser. Today's customary ascent, by the North-West Face and the West Ridge (photo p.57), has more glacier work and an exposed summit ridge slope. This way is more serious but is greatly shortened by the cableway to Hohsaas.

An early departure from the hut offers the advantage of hard snow and the experience of the dawn hours, with the better chance of distant visibility from the summit before the thermals produce clouds to obscure the view. Alternatively, those who wish to bag this mountain in a single day, can travel up on the first cable car, but will then be forced to rush before the snow becomes rotten – a race which one always loses in fine weather.

Difficulties: PD. Snow or ice, to 40°, with some exposure.
Effort: From Hohsaas to the summit 1050mH in 3-4 hrs ascent. The worse part of the ascent to the hut can be avoided by using the cableway.
Dangers: Occasional falling ice shortly after setting foot on the glacier and at the foot of the North-West Face. On the glacier there is some crevasse danger (mostly obvious, and there is almost always a worn track which makes things much easier, especially on the exposed summit ridge. Here there are big cornices all the way to the summit.
Pleasures: Impressive glacier scenery and, in good visibility, a fantastic panoramic view.

Maps: LKS 1329 Saas, LKS 5006 Matterhorn-Mischabel.
Travel: By rail up the Rhône valley to Visp and on to Stalden, from there 14km by bus. By car from Visp (Rhône valley) via Stalden and up the Saas valley 21km to *Saas Grund*

(1559m) a tourist resort with all the trimmings, also campsites and a tourist office.

Hut climb: Take the cableway via Kreuzboden (2397m) to the *Hohsaashaus* (3098m) on the ridge above and north of the Trift Glacier. There is a hut by the mountain station (Saas Grund Community, 36 B, managed from the end of June to early October, Tel. 028-57 18 22). Alternatively, go to Kreuzboden (Chrizbode) and take a good path to the *Weissmies Huts* (45 mins) situated under big moraines (2726m, SAC, 124 B, managed from mid-July to the end of September, Tel. 028-57 25 54).

Those who spurn the temptation of the cableway or who miss it, can also ascend from Unter dem Berg, taking a path from north of the town centre, which leads, with many zig-zags, to Triftalp (2072m). It continues up, near the Triftbach, to the Kreuzboden and the hut (1540mH, 5-6 hrs).

Summit route: From the Weissmies Huts take the path over the moraine ridges above, heading south to the Hohsaashaus (45 mins).

From there ascend east-south-east on the flat ridge to gain a crude man-made ramp leading down the Trift Glacier. Climb this, firstly through a bare crevasse zone, to a flatter section and then up over a steep snow slope. To avoid broad crevasses ahead, turn right and then continue up the face to the south-east. Before reaching the West Summit (P.3820) trend left to gain a saddle on the West Ridge. Keep left of the corniced ridge, on the face (exposed and without rock belays) to eventually reach the summit.

View: To the south are the Portjengrat, the Stellihorn and Monte Rosa, to the west the whole long ridge crest from the Strahlhorn to the Nadelhorn. The nearby Lagginhorn dominates to the north with the distant Bernese Alps beyond. To the east are wild views down into the Zwischenbergen and Laggin valleys as well as, in the distance, the Engadine and Bernina ranges.

Adjacent peaks: The not-very-independent West Summit (3820m) can be reached with a short excursion from the saddle on the West Ridge.

Other worthwhile routes: *The South Face and South-East Ridge (Original Route)* from the Almageller Hut, 2860m; (PD, climbing to I, little snow, 1180 mH to the hut plus 1140mH ascent, 7-8 hrs from the hut).

North Ridge (D, IV– and III, finally snow, 6-10 hrs from Hohsaas).

Guidebook: Pennine Alps East (The Alpine Club, 1975).

This ridge, running south to the frontier crest, is defined and accessed by the two big flanking valleys, the Saas valley only by road, and the Matter valley by road and rail. This single crest of peaks boasts over a dozen 4000ers.

The northern part of this ridge bears the name 'Mischabel', which sounds rather exotically Swiss, but nevertheless means quite prosaically and unkindly 'Mistgabel' (dung fork). In this part of the range there is only one cableway (not very conveniently placed) and climbing by one's own efforts is trumps and the atmosphere correspondingly sportsmanlike.

Dürrenhorn, 4035m
Hohberghorn, 4219m
Nadelhorn, 4327m

The most northerly 4000er of the mighty ridge crest between the Saas valley and the Matter valley is the Dürrenhorn. In the famous traverse of the entire Nadelgrat it is the first or last summit. An ascent of this peak alone involves a route with very long approach. For that reason, it is better combined with a round that includes the Hohberghorn and Stecknadelhorn (which likewise would scarcely be climbed otherwise) as well as the dominating Nadelhorn. The first ascent of the complete Nadelgrat (from the Dom Hut over the Hohberghorn to the Lenzspitze and back to the Dom Hut) was made in 1892 under the leadership of the well-known Engadine guide Christian Klucker. The first traverse from the Lenzspitze to the Galenjoch and on over the Galengrat, was done in 1916 by Adrian Mazlam with the well-known guide Josef Knubel. The individual first ascents were as follows: the Dürrenhorn – Albert Frederick Mummery (who, after fierce Alpine climbs, was to die in 1895 on Nanga Parbat) and William Penhall with Alexander Burgener and Ferdinand Imseng in September 1879; the Hohberghorn – by R.B. Heathcote with Franz

On the northern part of the Nadelgrat: Hohberghorn (left) and Stecknadelhorn.

Biner (Weisshorn-Biner), Peter Perren and Peter Taugwalder in 1869; the Stecknadelhorn – by Oscar Eckenstein (later to become well-known as the designer of crampons) with Matthias Zurbriggen (later to conquer Aconcagua) in August 1887.

On this traverse, it is worth considering carefully which is the best direction for the expedition. If one begins the route at the Nadelhorn (starting from the Mischabel Hut), then its sharply cut North-East Ridge lies in the magic of the morning light and one can usually reach the summit before the clouds build up. The defect in this strategy is that there is something of an anticlimax on the following summits and a tiring conclusion as the return will be over the softened Ried Glacier. If the excursion is to be started in the opposite direction, then the Ried Glacier will still be in crisp condition for an early traverse. The Dürrenhorn ascent in the morning sun is thrilling, and after that the airy – and increasingly firm ridge to the Nadelhorn provides a fitting climax. The descent over the North-East Ridge may then be soft but has the advantage of being well-defined (helpful in poor visability) and leaving no re-ascent at the end of the day. Naturally, the merits and demerits of these strategies offer an opportunity for argument when planning the climb in the hut. However, there is one thing over which there will be no argument.

The weather must be really reliable for the traverse of such a long and remote ridge. A popular, shorter version of the ridge that avoids the Reid Glacier return is to traverse the Nadelhorn to the Hohberghorn and then return over the Nadelhorn. That of course leaves the Dürrenhorn unclimbed.

Difficulties: AD. The principal difficulties of the route usually lie in the ascent up the steep couloir to the Hohbergjoch (especially late in summer, often big bergschrund; in bad snow or ice the steep couloir is avoidable on the crumbling rocks north of it). On the ridge between Dürrenhorn and Nadelhorn there is a pitch of II+, otherwise II– and I, mixed, partly also snow ridges. The descent of Nadelhorn North-East Ridge is II– and I, mixed.

Effort: The hut climb involves a wretched 1550mH (4-5 hrs in the sun until mid-day) direct from Saas Fee or travel on the cableway to the Hannigalpe, 2349m. which still leaves 1000mH (3-4 hrs); the summit route to Dürrenhorn by the detour over Ulrichshorn and the Riedpass involves 1000mH (4-5 hrs) or by the more direct approach from the Windjoch to the Hohbergjoch Couloir 600mH, but this way can be crevassed. From the Hohbergjoch to Nadelhorn is a further 500mH ascent (3-4 hrs). The descent from the Nadelhorn to the hut is 1000mH (2 hrs).

Dangers: Both Hohbalm Glacier and Ried Glacier are replete with unpleasant crevasses, but by using the detour over the Ulrichshorn and Riedpass the most prominent crevasse zones are bypassed. On the ascent to the Hohbergjoch there is stone-fall potential. Beware of cornices on the ridge itself.

Pleasures: An especially scenic and impressive ridge traverse that is amongst the most famous in the Western Alps.

Maps, travel, hut climb (and on to Windjoch): see Nadelhorn.
Summit route with a finish over the Nadelhorn: climb to the Windjoch 3850m (1 hr from the Mischabel Huts). From here, in good conditions, make a direct approach to the Hohbergjoch Couloir by a traverse of the steep, upper Ried Glacier. For that it is best to climb for a short distance towards the Nadelhorn looking for a route working round above the prominent ice-fall to gain the foot of the couloir. Alternatively, take the more circuitous but easier route over the South-West Ridge of the Ulrichshorn, 3925m, and

north-eastwards to the Riedpass. Now traverse west across the wide, flat basin of the Ried Glacier to the foot of the Hohbergjoch Couloir south of the Dürrenhorn. Cross the often problematical bergschrund and either climb the 45° snow or take the rocks on the right to gain the Hohbergjoch (3916m; 4-5 hrs from the Mischabel huts).

From the col the **Dürrenhorn** (4035m) can be climbed quickly using the brittle rocks of the South-East Ridge (II and I) with a return to Hohbergjoch (1 hr).

Now climb the ridge south-eastwards, first over rocks, then up the broad snow ridge to a rocky rise. Turn this on the left or climb it directly (II) and follow a snow ridge to the summit of the **Hohberghorn** (4219m). Continue east-south-east on the snow ridge down into the Stecknadeljoch (4142m, 2 hrs from Hohbergjoch). The rocky pinnacle ridge above is passed on the right on rising ledges (II– and I) to reach the less prominent summit of the **Stecknadelhorn** (4241m, 2-3 hrs from the Hohbergjoch).

Descend over rock into a snow saddle and over a snow ridge to a gendarme. Climb this direct (II+) or turn it (often bare ice) to reach a snow notch behind. From there it is a short distance further on the North-East Ridge to the summit of the Nadelhorn (4327m, 3-4 hrs from Hohbergjoch). For descent, see Nadelhorn.

Other worthwhile routes: *The complete Nadelgrat* from the Dom Hut over the Lenzspitze and the Nadelhorn and on to the Dürrenhorn (AD, an exuberant whole day's expedition, or more).

Dürrenhorn North Ridge from the Galenjoch (AD, III and II, brittle, long approach or descent, belongs to the gluttons' greater traverse of the entire Nadelgrat).

Hohberghorn North-East Face (AD, 350mH, up to 50° ice).

Hohberghorn and/or Stecknadelhorn from west (PD, 5 hrs from the Dom Hut via Festijoch, the Hohberg Glacier and the Stecknadeljoch Couloir (afternoon stone-fall) is a technically easier but not the usual approach).

Guidebook: Pennine Alps East (The Alpine Club, 1975).

Nadelhorn, 4327m

The highest summit of the ridge crest north of the Dom sends out three prominent ridges. Between them, rocky gneiss faces made up of steep gullies and ribs fall to the south-east and south-west, while the somewhat concave North Face is partially clad in an impressive shield of ice. This mountain is also still only reachable on foot (apart from a short initial lift from Saas Fee). The first ascent was made in September 1858 by the labourers Joseph Zimmermann, Alois Supersaxo and Baptist Epiney, led by the guide Franz Andermatten, in order to erect a trig point. They are approached by the Windjoch and the elegant North-East Ridge which today is still the ordinary route.

Difficulties: PD. On the rocky sections of the ridge, some pitches of II–, mostly I, mixed, with snow to 40°.
Effort: To the Mischabel Hut from Saas Fee 1550mH ascent (4-5 hrs), from Hannigalp 1000mH (3-4 hrs). Summit climb 1000mH.
Dangers: An objectively safe route. On the Hohbalm Glacier there are some crevasses but these present no problems with correct choice of route. There are cornices on the ridge.
Pleasures: The ridge is an ideal line, practical as guide-line for route-finding, helpful for belaying, free of stone-fall and with the great symbolic power of a direct line to the highest point in the sky.

Maps: LKS 1328 Randa, also LKS 5006 Matterhorn-Mischabel. See Lenzspitze and Dom sketches.
Travel: By rail to Stalden, from there by bus 18km via Saas Grund (see Weissmies) up to Saas Fee (1792m; very exclusive tourist resort which above all belongs to pedestrians because it deprives drivers of their vehicles at the outskirts of the town incarcerating them in a multi-storey garage).
Hut climb: Through the town and from Leeboden, ascend westwards to the avalanche barrier at the Torrenbach. Go through a tunnel and over the stream. After that, to the broad track which leads, with a daunting number of bends, up the slope of the Trift to P.2448 on the South-East Ridge of the Distelhorn.

Descending the Eselsrucken on the Gran Paradiso.

‹‹ Gran Paradiso's East Peak from the Madonna summit.

A pair of Ibex, high on the slopes of Gran Paradiso.

Crossing Pic Lory on the Barre des Écrins – the narrowest part of the summit ridge. The main summit is on the lower left.

The view from below the Glacier Noir across the 1000-metre South Face of the Barre des Écrins (right) to Pic Coolidge (left).

An eastern panorama from P.3718 on the North-East Ridge of the Aletschhorn to the Fiescherhorner (left), the Gross-Grünhorn and the Finsteraarhorn.

On the Aletsch Glacier, the mightiest and longest ice stream in the Alps, which flows south from the heart of the Bernese Oberland.

The summit slopes of the Aletschhorn from P.3718 on the North-East Ridge at the point where the Hasler Rib exits from the North Face.

Gross-Grünhorn from south-west, from the fore-summit of the Grünegghorn.

‹ *Looking north to the Gross-Fiescherhorn from the ridge to the Hinter-Fiescherhorn.*

Nearing the top of the Grünegghorn on the South-West Ridge.

Gross-Grünhorn and Hinter-Fiescherhorn from the Finsteraarhorn Hut.

Finsteraarhorn from the Finsteraarhorn Hut. The ordinary route leads obliquely left across the glacier.

The Finsteraar Hut, one of the remotest in the Bernese Oberland.

Evening sunlight bathes the North-West Face of the Weissmies as seen from the Hohsaas Hut.

On the Weissmies Glacier.

The final section of the West Ridge of the Weissmies.

A panorama looking west from the Hohsaas Hut to the Allalin group and Mischabel group.

Täschhorn and Dom from the Metro at Mittelallalin.

The Allalinhorn from south-east, from the Ofental.

The view back from P.3837 on the Hohlaubgrat of the Allalinhorn.

The steep slope above P.3597 on the Hohlaubgrat.

The summit block of the Allalinhorn from the top of the Hohlaubgrat.

On the upper part of the East Ridge of the Weisshorn. ››

On the northern slope of the Feejoch.

Continue up the ridge until the path leads further left (west) in the direction of the Fall Glacier. Before reaching this, go right (north) steeply up over rock (wire cables) and finally, over a less steep slope, to the *Mischabel Huts* (3329m and 3340m, SAC, AACZ, 120 B, managed in summer, Tel. 028-57 13 17).

(The route from the cableway terminus at Hannigalpe takes an indistinct ski descent southwards and after 150 metres moves right on a narrow path descending slightly to the valley of the Torrenbach. This is crossed by a bridge and the path then continues under the East Face of the Distelhorn to P.2448 to join the main Saas Fee ascent path.

Summit route: From the huts, ascend the moraine ridge near the Hohbalm Glacier until at about 3600m this becomes more level and tamer. Traverse the glacier northwards (good view of the North-East Face of the Lenzspitze) and ascend over a somewhat steeper snow-slope (crevasses), first keeping right below the Ulrichshorn, then moving across left to go up to the Windjoch (3850m; 1-2 hrs from the Mischabel Huts).

Climb the initially broad, but soon narrowing snow ridge. Continue above over rocky rises (turnable in part on right), then keep directly on the ridge line to the summit block with slight deviations on the left near the top. (3-4 hrs from the huts).

View: To the south the nearby Lenzspitze and the mighty Dom interrupt the distant view, but there is a wide panorama to the west to the intriguing Weisshorn group. To the north, behind the continuation of the Nadelgrat, there is the more distant Bernese Oberland and the Weissmies group is to the east.

Descent by the ordinary route: From the summit, climb down north-eastwards following the crampon scratches and near the ridge edge, and keep on the ridge edge down to the Windjoch. Descend from this on the south side and over the flat snow of the Hohbalm Glacier to its south side. There, on the rock ridge, go left down to the Mischabel Huts.

Other worthwhile routes: *Nadelgrat* to the Dürrenhorn, see above.

South-East Ridge (from the Lenzspitze over the Nadeljoch, first and most beautiful part of the entire Nadelgrat – AD, III in dry condition but, when icy, it becomes very hard, 4 hrs from the Lenzspitze).

Guidebook: Pennine Alps East (The Alpine Club, 1975).

Lenzspitze, 4294m

The most southerly summit of the Nadelgrat is, like the Nadelhorn, one of the typical three-sided gneiss pyramids. From the Saas side, it is conspicuous by the steep ice shield of its North-East Face. In recent years this has occasionally revealed some dry patches of rock. The first ascent was made in 1870 by Clinton Dent with Alexander and Franz Burgener who climbed the steep North-East Face to the Nadeljoch and from there along the North-West Ridge. Today's customary ordinary routes are the East-North-East Ridge, whose first ascent fell to Ambros Supersaxo and Theodor Andenmatten with W.W. Graham in 1882, and the South Ridge from the Lenzjoch which Ambros Supersaxo and L. Zurbriggen with R.F. Ball first climbed in 1888.

The usual descent is the traverse of the pinnacle ridge to the Nadelhorn (southern Nadelgrat – only advisable in good conditions and reliable weather) and descent over its North-East Ridge, resulting in a considerable round trip.

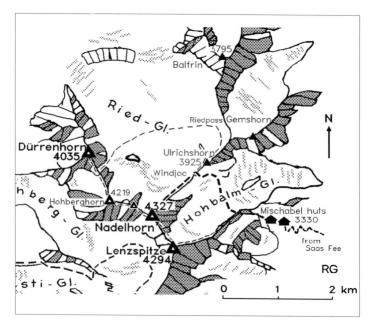

Difficulties: East-North-East Ridge (AD, with sustained, mixed climbing at II and I and several pitches of III). South-West Ridge from the Lenzjoch (PD with II+ and II). The traverse to the Nadelhorn along the southern Nadelgrat (AD, an exposed alpine ridge with constant up and down passages with some pitches of III, all of which can become troublesome if heavily iced up).

Effort: From the Mischabel Huts to the summit 950mH ascent (4-5 hrs), from the Dom Hut 1350mH (5-6 hrs). The traverse over the Nadelhorn c.200mH (2-3 hrs), then 1000mH descent (2 hrs).

Dangers: Beware of cornices on the ridges. In the upper part of the North-East Ridge and on the South-West Ridge there is some brittle rock, but generally both are objectively safe climbs in good conditions, but in high winds or storms they can become very tricky. In really bad weather even strong parties will find it hard to cope with such exposed ridges at this height!

Pleasures: The rock on the hard pitches of the North-East Ridge and on the Nadelgrat is firm giving delectable sections of climbing all slightly harder than anything on the northern Nadelgrat.

Maps, travel, hut climbs: See Nadelhorn and Dom. For sketches, see also Dom.

Summit routes from the Mischabel Hut by the East-North-East Ridge: Head west along a path up rounded rocks past the branching of the track to the Windjoch, and keep on the ridge to P.3815. (This point can also be reached by first ascending the Hohbalm Glacier and then gaining the ridge by a snow gully.)
After a horizontal section, the ridge steepens. Climb the first steep rise on the north side and then continue along the sharp, often corniced, ridge to the first tower. Climb a slab until one can traverse right to a crack. On this to a ledge, then go obliquely left towards a recess and up steps to the ridge above. The ridge continues more easily to a notch and to the foot of Grand Gendarme which overhangs on the south-side. Avoid the flank and climb its prominent big slab on the left (piton). On the other side, climb or abseil down the difficult five-metre crack. Continue along the following horizontal section of ridge to the third rise. This is taken on its edge, steeply but on good holds and then zig-zags, partly on the knife-edge, partly beside it, to the snow ridge. This joins the South Ridge and leads on to the summit.

On descent, the steeper parts of the rock pinnacles or little tops can be abseiled (possibly renewing slings!).

From the Dom Hut via the South Ridge: This follows the same approach as the ordinary route to the Dom until below the Lenzjoch. Go up a steepening snow slope trending left to cross the bergschrund and then climb up into the notch left (north) of the lowest col, left of several pinnacles. The ridge is first of all predominantly on snow, but this becomes more rocky leading up to a big, pointed gendarme that is turned on the right (Saas side) and the ridge regained. Continue with decreasing difficulty and finally ascend to the summit by a gully on the west side.

Traverse to the Nadelhorn (southern Nadelgrat): On the ridge falling away north-westwards, descend over snow (occasionally delicate, beware of cornices) and some rock into the Nadeljoch (4213m). After that, continue on the rocky ridge, either by steady up and down work over the ridge towers on good holds, or by turning the towers as conditions allow. From the Nadeljoch traverse the first tower on its south edge on the right (east) as far as the overhang, and up over a slab on good small holds to the notch. Traverse the second tower at half height on the east and up a little wall to the ridge. Descend over slabs to the next notch. Continue on the ridge. The next, bigger, gendarme is climbed direct and then descended to a low notch. From this go directly on the knife-edge to the summit of the Nadelhorn (for view and descent, see Nadelhorn.)

Other worthwhile routes: *North-East Face or Dreieselswand* (D, a classic ice face with sections of 55°, 4-6hrs, 500mH).

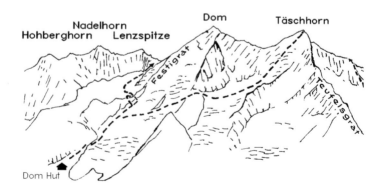

Dom, 4545m

This is the highest mountain lying wholly inside Switzerland. From the east and south-west it is seen as the highest in a row of pointed gneiss pyramids, but from the north-west it seems merely a little white cloud set between the green of the high alps and the blue sky. The name is logical on account of its height or its prominent shape or also on account of its majestic icy north face. It was named, however, after the surveyor Domherr Berchthold of Sion. Its first ascent was made on 11 September 1858 by J.L. Davies with Johann Zumtaugwald, Johann Kronig and Hieronymous Brantschen by the North-West Ridge or Festigrat. The easiest climb is, by contrast, the North Face, notorious as a miserable snow plod, but on account of the overwhelming monotony of its enormous dimensions still an impressive undertaking.

Difficulties: PD. On approach to the Festijoch there are some pitches to II, but otherwise a glacier ascent, practically without technical difficulties. The Festigrat is PD+ with snow or ice up to 50°.

Effort: Hut climb 1510mH (5-6 hrs, best tackled in the early morning shade), summit climb 1650mH (5-7 hrs).

Dangers: The Dom is noted for its high altitude storms. On the traverse of the Hohberg Glacier move quickly keeping a sensible distance from the sérac zone, where there is often ice debris. Otherwise, the customary glacier precautions are advisable. In mist and in storm or with driving snow covering tracks, route-finding can quickly become very problematical.

Pleasures: A very remote area with no cableways and therefore people are, through the efforts of the ascent, correspondingly hand-picked.

Maps: LKS 1328 Randa, also LKS 5006 Matterhorn-Mischabel. See also Lenzspitze topo.

Travel: By rail up the Matter valley to Randa, a gratifyingly quiet tourist resort (camping; also bus route). By car – 23km from Visp in the Rhône valley.

Hut climb: From Randa, past the church, go north-east to the Dorfbach. Before reaching this, climb up through the wood on the south side and cross the torrent at about 1900m and ascend on the other side to the tree-line. Continue up the bends, over pasture slopes to a high rock barrier. Up this over steps, gullies and ledges (some wire ropes) to a small rock plateau and move up debris to the north bank moraine of the Festi Glacier. Continue along this to the Dom Hut which was originally built in the form of a mountain crystal, (2940m, SAC Section Uto, 75 B, Self-cooking room and winter room, managed from mid-July to the end of August, Tel. 028-67 26 34).

Summit route: From the hut, continue along the moraine for about 30 mins to the Festi Glacier. Ascend the northern edge of this for another 30 mins to reach the area below the Festijoch. Before reaching this, cut up the hill west of the fall line, following cairns over the ridge of a small black tower to gain the main ridge between the Festi and Hohberg Glaciers. Traverse steep rocks on the south side into a small notch, then cross to the north side and follow an exposed, rising ledge (II) to a stance and thence down to the Festijoch (3723m, 2-3 hrs from the Dom Hut. This col is also reachable directly from the Festi Glacier (II and I).

Now descend somewhat northwards to the Hohberg Glacier (section of steep ice and a bergschrund) and, keeping a respectful distance from the sérac zone, traverse swiftly across

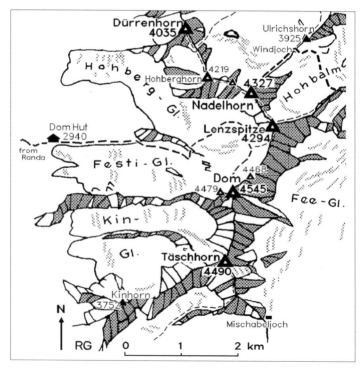

A view from the Nadelgrat of the North-West Face of the Dom with the Festigrat on the right.

to under the faces of the Hohberghorn and Stecknadelhorn. From this safer region, climb up the glacier to below the Lenzjoch. Now head southwards over the interminable glacier slopes in the direction of the saddle between the western foresummit and the main summit of the Dom. From the saddle continue to the highest point (5-7 hrs from the hut).

View: From here one can make a detailed inspection of the rocky gneiss faces of the Nadelgrat to the north, to the south is the nearby Täschhorn, to the east the Saas valley and Weissmies, to the south-east the alien element of the summer ski circus north of the Allalinhorn. To the west the splendid Weisshorn, to the south-west the Matterhorn.

Adjacent peaks: The **western fore-summit P.4479** is quickly climbed from the ordinary route. The **North-East Ridge Summit P.4468** is reachable with a somewhat bigger detour from the ordinary route without undue difficulty.

Other worthwhile routes: *Festigrat* (from the Festijoch go directly up the little marked North-West Ridge, PD+, II, in the higher section keeping mostly to the north of the knife-edge on snow, 3 hrs from the Festijoch).

North-East Ridge (above the Lenzjoch, the lower part to P.4468 has difficulties up to IV+, after that there is easier snow work, TD, 3-5 hrs from the Lenzjoch).

South Ridge (III, worthwhile as part of the traverse from the Täschhorn but horribly long and at a great height).

West Ridge (IV, seldom climbed, 8 hrs).

Guidebook: Pennine Alps East (The Alpine Club, 1975).

Täschhorn, 4490m

Seen from the south, the Täschhorn totally upstages the higher Dom, not only because it hides it, but because its rugged South Face holds the attention. There is no comparable face in this part of the Alps. Its first ascent by Franz and Josef Lochmatter with V.J.E. Ryan and Geoffrey Winthrop Young with Josef Knubel in 1906, using the rudimentary equipment of that time, remains one of the most unbelievable deeds of Alpine history (and Young's chapter, 'A Memory of the Mischabel' from *On High Hills*, one of the most thrilling descriptions in Alpine literature). This is one of the more difficult 4000 metre peaks. All the climbs are demanding in one way or another: the North-West Face, up which the first ascent was made in 1862 has difficulties (and risks) on the ice. The South-East Ridge (Mischabelgrat), climbed in 1876 by J. Jackson with the guides Christian and Ulrich Almer, is also quite tricky. These days, however, after the building of the Mischabeljoch bivouac, it is treated as the ordinary route. The South-West Ridge (Teufelsgrat), which is almost 2km long, was climbed by Joseph Andenmatten with A.F. Mummery and Mrs M. Mummery in 1887, is AD+ and not of high quality.

Difficulties: The South-East Ridge is AD with pitches of III, though generally easier, but long. The start is somewhat brittle and on the middle part of the snow ridge and particularly on the snow shoulder there are cornices. The ideal conditions are not too snowy and not too dry (when the ridge becomes unstable). The North-West Face (AD) is a steep glacier with very variable difficulties according to conditions, often with passages of steep ice climbing, as well as rock up to II+. In addition there can be route-finding problems because the mountain is not frequently climbed and one cannot count on having a track to follow – a particularly relevant consideration if the face is to be used for descent. Indeed there is no easy descent from this peak, an important factor if bad weather threatens.

Effort: The climb to the Täsch Hut involves 1300mH (4 hrs), then 1700mH ascent to the summit (7-9 hrs). From the Dom Hut by the Festi-Kin-Lücke and North-West Face 1700mH allow 6 hrs.

Dangers: In addition to the aforementioned problems there are crevasses on the approach on the Weingarten Glacier.

Pleasures: On the summit block there is enjoyable climbing on firm gneiss in a fantastic position. The satisfaction of climbing a remote and difficult 4000er, where one finds oneself in exclusive company or none at all.

Maps: LKS 1328 Randa, also LKS 5006 Matterhorn-Mischabel. For sketches, see Dom, Lenzspitze, Alphubel.

Travel: By rail from Visp/Rhône Valley up the Matter Valley (31km) to Tasch (1449m, tourist resort, also campsites and gigantic car-park at the end of the motor road).

Hut climbs: From Täsch, north of the Täschbach, take the path up to Täschberg (1696m) and continue to Eggenstadel (1950). Before reaching the bridge take a path up the steep slope north of the stream to the upper Täschalp. Here there is accommodation at Ottavan, (2214m, private, 15 B) which can be reached by car up the back road from Täsch, or by a long traversing route from the south using the mountain station of Sunegga (2288m). Continue steeply on the broad track rising up the north side of the valley to the Täsch Hut at the foot of the Rotgrat descending from the Alphubel (2701m, SAC-Section Uto, 60 B, managed from June to September, Tel. 028-67 9 13).

Summit route from the Täsch Hut by the South-West Rib and the upper part of the South-East Ridge: Head north-westwards from the hut along a good track that passes under the rocks of the Rotgrat. Beyond that, climb eastwards up the Tälli Cwm. Before reaching P.3195 work north and cross the Wissgrat and descend a stone staircase to the broad moraine fields of the Weingarten Glacier. Continue north between the southern part of the glacier and a lake and pass below P.3242 and P.3223 at the foot of two ridges descending from the Alphubel and cross below a heavily crevassed section of the glacier to gain the foot of a spur descending west from the South-East Ridge of the Täschhorn. Climb this, first over debris and snow, then steeper but without any major difficulty, passing P.3633, to finally join the South-East Ridge about halfway between the Mischabeljoch and the summit, somewhat south of P.4175.

Climb the broad ridge to a couloir descending to the east. Here the ridge becomes a snow edge, the east side of which is heavily corniced. At a steep snow/ice shoulder traverse along a ledge the on the west side and then climb steep ice to regain the crest of the ridge after which two more pitches on ice or snow lead to the foot of the final pyramid. Move up right to rocks which give enjoyable solid climbing that leads straight to the summit.

The lower, more friable, section of the South-East Ridge can also be climbed with moderate difficulties direct from the

Mischabeljoch. But in good weather the bivouac hut may be unpleasantly crowded. However, if a traverse to the Dom is planned it is best to start from here. This is conveniently reached by an approach over the Alphubel (see pages 93 and 94) making use of the Metro or the cableway. The Täsch approach reaches the crevassed upper Weingarten Glacier by a route using the notch at P.3481.

Summit climb from the Dom Hut by the North-West Face: A fine route, best tackled in good snow conditions to minimise the crevasse and step-cutting problems. Follow the same approach as for the ordinary route to the Dom to below the Festijoch. Now traverse the Festi Glacier under the rock island with P.3781 and up a steepening slope (55° often icy, bergschrund often large) to the Festi-Kin-Lücke (3734m, 2-3 hrs from the Dom Hut; in good snow conditions one can start the traverse earlier at 3400m, and ascend south-eastwards). Move up the lower part of the West Ridge of the Dom for about 100mH (to where the ground below the Dom Hut is again visible), then work obliquely downwards on ledges to the northern Kin Glacier and make a rising traverse across the snow basin to the North-West Face of the Täschhorn (3-4 hrs from the Dom Hut). The face is really a very confusing glacier with constantly changing topography. For this reason a detailed description is pointless. Work a way up as conditions dictate but in the final section move right to finish up the Teufelsgrat.

View: To the north is the nearby Dom with its rock and ice faces and to the south-east the lower Alphubel and Allalinhorn and to the south the whole of the head of the Zermatt Valley. To the east is the Weissmies group and to the west the Weisshorn group.

Adjacent peaks: The not very prominent **North Ridge Summit P.4404** is passed on the ridge traverse to the Dom. The **South-East Ridge Summit P.4175** is traversed during the ascent.

Other worthwhile routes: *The Täschhorn-Dom traverse* (AD+, III and II, but mostly narrow and airy, in part corniced, very long and high, 3-5 hrs from summit to summit). The value of this route, apart from its obvious classic stature, is that it gives access to the easier descent of the Dom.

South-West Ridge or Teufelsgrat (D, IV, very long, 12-15 hrs).
South-West Face (TD+, 900mH, 10-15 hrs, a piece of alpine history, not beautiful but prestigious because it is so rarely climbed. Loose and dangerous and regarded as a 'horror show'.

Guidebook: Pennine Alps East (The Alpine Club, 1975).

In the Mischabel group an almost rectilinear ridge crest dominates the scene. However, south of that the character of the landscape changes. The glacier basins extend further and the crest line is more broken up.

The 4000ers tower up but they are more rounded and easily accessed using mountain railways or cableways that adorn both the eastern and western slopes. Thus these mountains are good for quick ascents but offer a less satisfying ambience than the remoter Mischabel peaks.

Alphubel, 4206m

A mountain with two very different faces. From the east a gigantic and apparently tedious snow hump, from the west a rugged rock peak with walls and buttressed ridges. On closer inspection the east side appears not as harmless as at first glance and in recent years the opening crevasses on the Fee Glacier have often made the climbing caravans work hard to make an ascent from that quarter.

On this eastern flank the Alphubel can be approached by both rail and cableway, the former by the tunnel railway (Métro) to the Mittelallalin, the latter using the transportation to Langflue. Although the Metro has provided another possible approach it has, nevertheless, the disadvantage that there are no possibilities for passing the night there and thus without a bivouac no really early departure is possible. For that reason, the ascent of the old route up the Alphubel using Langflue followed by a descent to the Feejoch and thence down to Mittelallalin is described.

The first ascent of the Alphubel was made in 1860 from Täsch over the Alphubeljoch and the South-East Ridge by the then 28-year old Leslie Stephen (who called the Alps the 'Playground of Europe' thereby anticipating the development of Alpinism, tourism and tourist traffic), T.W. Hinchliff and the guides Melchior Anderegg and Peter Perren. This climb is also the easiest route for all for who regard the unassisted (cableway-free) ascents of the 4000ers as a matter of honour.

Difficulties: PD. Normally the east side is a snow plod, also beloved as a ski excursion, but later in the season, crevasses must be reckoned with. On the ridge from the Feejoch there are few crevasse problems, but instead there is a 50-metre mixed passage (II) to surmount on the climb to the Feechopf. In addition the upper part of the South-East Ridge (Eisnase 45°) is often icy. In bad visibility the route-finding on the south-east route is more difficult and the highest point on the summit plateau is quite hard to locate.

Effort: Hut climb to the Langflue 1170mH (in view of the presence of the seductive cableway scarcely anyone does this), from there 1330mH (4-5 hrs) snaking through the crevasse system to the summit. Descent to Mittelallalin and to the Métro alpin 860mH, plus 110mH in the opposite direction (2-3 hrs).

Dangers: The best way to cope with the crevasses on the Fee Glacier is by starting very early and this allows a return by the same route before the snow becomes soft. In bad visibility, and if a wind covers over the track, there can be serious route-finding problems.

Pleasures: The south-east route offers wonderful views on descent or ascent in total contrast to the skiing bedlam of the upper Fee Glacier in which a mountaineer seems totally out of place.

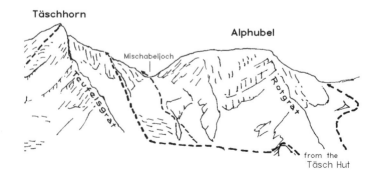

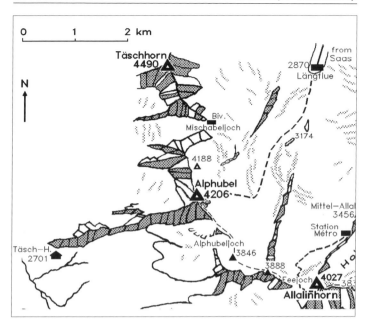

Maps, travel, guidebooks: See Nadelhorn and Täschhorn.

Hut climb: Through Saas Fee, past the conspicuous red tennis courts, visible even from the high summits and hideously intrusive, and the valley station of the Felskinn Railway and on an old central moraine of the Fee Glacier (Gletscheralp) under the cableway up to the Spielboden (2447m, mid-way station of the cableway from Saas Fee). Continue up the path in bends to a rock step and after that over debris terrain to the mountain station of the cableway and to the Bergsteigerheim Langflue (2870m, private, 220 B, managed all year, Tel. 028-57 21 32).

Summit route from Langflue: Head south-south-westwards and southwards across the Fee Glacier past the rock island P.3173.7, passing through some crevasse zones. Always keep a respectful distance from the mighty slanting rock wall of the Alphubel's North-East Spur which is often impressively animated by ice avalanches. From about 3600m one ascends directly over the steepening eastern slopes, often with a big crevasse at 4000m, to the extensive summit plateau and the highest point.

Alphubel from Mittelallalin.

Descent by Alphubeljoch-Feechopf-Feejoch to Mittelallalin:
From the main summit, first of all reverse the ordinary route
eastwards until under the upper-most steep slope and then
with a long, somewhat descending traverse southwards (or,
more difficult, go directly down the often icy South-East Ridge)
proceed to the Alphubeljoch (3782m). Head south over the flat
top of P.3846, then go east to a saddle and up the slope to the
prominent Feechopf (3888m). Now continue somewhat more
delicately on the ridge (II) down into the Feejoch (3826m; a
detour to take in the Allalinhorn is possible here). From the
Feejoch a broad highway leads down to the Métro at Mittelallalin.

Adjacent peaks: The **North Summit P.4188** is a flat top some
500m north of the highest point. The 300m further away
P.4128, occasionally designated as the North-East Summit, is
only a snow shoulder.

Other worthwhile routes: *South-East Ridge from the west*
(easy as far as the often icy summit slope, 1500mH ascent,
4-5 hrs from the Täsch Hut; first ascent route).

West Ridge (Rotgrat) (AD, III and II, firm rock and mixed,
5-7 hrs from the Täsch Hut).

North Ridge (AD, III–, 1-2 hrs from the Mischabeljoch).

North Summit, West Ridge (D+, IV+, not wholly perfect rock
but objectively safe, 8-9 hrs from the Täsch Hut).

Allalinhorn, 4027m

The mountain railway has turned this into a very easy proposition. Its upper part, built in a tunnel (Métro alpin), is at least scenically acceptable being without masts and gondolas and their clattering and chattering. It is also maintenance friendly. From the window of the stepped cars one even gets an interesting insight into the structure of the rock, moulded by heat and pressure in the formation of the mountains. Nevertheless, the concentration of so many people in one spot is ecologically undesirable and the ski circus, with its noisy piste-making vehicles and the glacier basin blocked by lift masts, is brutal in the extreme. The track of the ordinary route leads through this area and only on the last few hundred metres does it assume the true character of a high alpine ascent. For that reason many people prefer to climb the mountain by the scenically grand Hohlaubgrat. Another tranquil route is by the South-West Ridge from the Allalinpass, by which the Saas pastor Johann Josef Imboden with Franz Josef Andenmatten and E.L. Ames made the first ascent of the peak in 1856, and which formerly served as the ordinary route. The Hohlaubgrat was first done in descent in 1882 by Heinrich Dubi with Alphons and Peter Supersaxo and first ascended in 1887 by H.W. Topham and G.H. Rendall with Aloys Supersaxo.

Difficulties: F. On the ordinary route, only snow (short pitches on crevasses to 50°, on the summit slope 40°, often with ice). On the Hohlaubgrat PD, before reaching the summit there is a 30mH rock step (II), otherwise there is only easy scrambling (I) and snow or ice to 40° (longer stretches).

Effort: On the ordinary route, from the Métro at Mittelallalin, there is 580mH ascent on broad track (2 hrs); to climb up to there from the valley on foot under the cableway and over the ski circus would not only demand severe physical effort, but also a high tolerance to aesthetic ugliness. On the scenically more beautiful and unspoiled Hohlaubgrat from the Britannia Hut, 1050mH ascent (4-5 hrs).

Dangers: On the first part of the ordinary route the main risk is of being run down by a speed-drunk skier. On ascent to the Feejoch there are some crevasses whose bridges might collapse under the thousandth passer-by. There is also the subjective danger, the temptation to the untrained and inexperienced to make the ascent without the necessary acclimatization and equipment. On the Hohlaubgrat, the rock step on the summit block is well protected with 3 large pitons.

Pleasures: For many people this is the only 4000er which they ever climb, or the last which they feel capable of, and so long as the numbers of mountains developed to such a degree remain rare, that is granted to them.

Maps and Travel: See Nadelhorn; for Britannia Hut, see also LKS 1329 Saas.

Hut climb: The ordinary route from the Mittelallalin does not require an overnight stop. The approach to the Hohlaubgrat starts at the Felskinn station (2991m). Go east across a big ramp in the glacier to the Egginerjoch and continue at roughly the same height to the *Britannia Hut* on the saddle between the Hinterallalin and the Kleiner Allalin (3030m, SAC, 113 B, managed February to October, Tel. 028-57 22 88).

Summit route from the Mittelallalin over the Feejoch: Cross the pistes heading south-west of the prominent spur over the initially steep glacier (some crevasses with steep upper lips) and then head up to the Feejoch (3826m). From the col climb the summit slope in a wide arc and then from the south-west gain the summit ridge and summit.

Summit route from the Britannia Hut by the East Ridge or Hohlaubgrat: Descend a path heading obliquely south-west, down to the Hohlaub Glacier. Ascend this keeping right (north-west) to turn a crevasse zone and then move left (south), gently rising to the rocky ridge. Continue on the ridge. In dry conditions this is entertaining but without difficulties (I).

After a steeper section taken on the left, keep close to the increasingly higher south-east cliffs (where the rock dries off soonest) to a steep snow or ice slope which goes over this to the ridge summit P.3597. Make a short but definite descent into

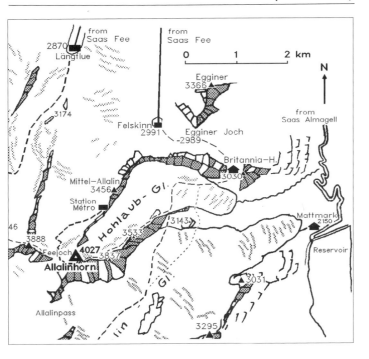

a saddle. (This point can be reached by a less interesting and more tiring ascent up the glacier to circumvent the lower part of the ridge). Continue up a long steep slope (often corniced on the left) to the east shoulder (P.3837), and over three shorter steep rises, with considerable views down the South Face, to the summit block. Climb a crack with good rough holds and over some steps (iron posts) to the eastern end of the summit ridge and a little further to the highest point.

View: A marvellous panorama with Mischabel group to the north-west and the nearby Rimpfischhorn and Strahlhorn to the south, as well as the already mentioned disfigurement on the north side.

Descent by the ordinary route: From the eastern end of the summit ridge at first descend south-westwards, but soon trend more to the right (west) and go down to the Feejoch. From there descend the steep glacier on the north side and then, on more gentle slopes, move right to the ski circus and the Métro (1 hr).

97

The Allalinhorn from Mittelallalin with the Hohlaubgrat on the left skyline.

Adjacent peaks: The East Ridge Summit P.3597 and the less prominent East Shoulder Summit P.3837 are quickly climbed on ascent over the Hohlaubgrat.

Other worthwhile routes: *South-West Ridge* (PD, from the Allalinpass – reachable from the Britannia Hut or from the Täsch Hut in 3 hrs – 500mH, 2 hrs, pitches of II).
North-East Ridge (AD+, direct from Métro, ice to 50°, 580mH, 3 hrs).
North-East Face (TD, extreme ice route left of the ridge, with a steep sérac zone with climbing from 60° to 90°, 430mH, 8 hrs).
South Face (AD+, rock to IV, mixed, 600mH, 4 hrs from starting climb).

Guidebook: Pennine Alps East (The Alpine Club, 1975).

Rimpfischhorn, 4199m

The pinnacled summit ridge, like the crest of a prehistoric giant reptile, is flanked to south-east and east by an (in summer) almost purely rock face, on the west by a mixed face. The length of the approach together with the climbing on the summit block, makes this one of the more exacting peaks of the region, even when one permits oneself the shortening of the hut climb by using the little railway.

The first ascent was made in 1859, by Leslie Stephen with his compatriot R. Liveing and the guides Melchior Anderegg and Johann Zumtaugwald by today's ordinary route.

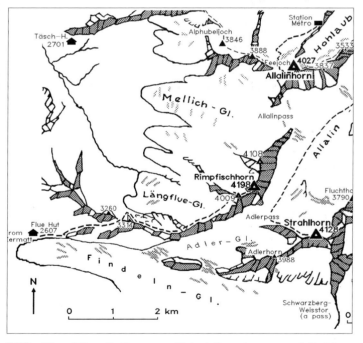

Difficulties: PD+. On the summit block there is exposed climbing, II+, otherwise II and I. In the couloir above the Rimpfischsattel there is ice climbing up to 50°, but up to that point the climb is predominantly a plod, with just 200mH of easy climbing (II and I, possibly also interspersed with snow) to P.4009.

Strahlhorn (left) and Rimpfischhorn (right) from the Hohlaubgrat.

Effort: The hut climb from Blauherd station of the Zermatt-Sunnegga-Unterrothorn railway involves about 80mH descent and ascent, 30 mins (by ascent on foot from Zermatt 1000mH, 3 hrs). The summit climb is then 1600mH (5-6 hrs).

Dangers: The ascent is objectively only mildly dangerous as it leads over an almost (!) crevasse-free snow ridge to the summit block. The summit rocks are often icy and in those conditions are very unfriendly.

Pleasures: Getting to grips with a beautifully shaped, rugged summit with a gradual increase in difficulty and exposure towards the summit. On the ridge edge of the fore-summit, 'gorgeous rock awaits'.

Maps: LKS 1348 Zermatt, LKS 5006 Matterhorn-Mischabel.

Travel: To Zermatt (1606m), see Dufourspitze.

Hut climb: From *Zermatt* head southwards to Winkelmatten. Then ascend eastwards, first of all close to the northern bank of the Findelbach. Later, keeping to the left, cross over the Gornergrat rack railway track and follow a forest path with many bends, up to Findeln (2051m).

Climb obliquely via Eggen (2177m) eastwards up the slopes of the Findelalp to the Stellisee (2537m) and continue to the *Berggasthaus Flue* (2618m, private, 20 + 30 B, managed in the ski and summer season, Tel. 028-67 25 51).

To here also from Zermatt by tunnel funicular railway to Sunnegga (2288m), from there by cableway to Blauherd (2560m) and south-eastwards down to the Stellisee, continue as above.

Summit route by the East Ridge: From Flue, head east for about 1km to small moraine lakes. The path now goes obliquely left up over the pasture and debris slopes of the Usseri Rimpfischwang and finally through a block labyrinth and over marl slopes or snow up to the Pfulwe saddle (3155m, between Spitzi Flue and Pfulwe). Traverse to the north of Pfulwe (3314m) to reach a not very prominent shoulder over a some-what low snow-field, and from this make a rising traverse over the North-East Face (crevasses) to the Langfluejoch (3270m). (This point can also be reached from the head of the valley above Täschalpe by a south-easterly line over moraines and the moraines and the lower Langfluh Glacier.)

Continue up the broad rock-studded ridge and later on the not very defined ridge edge (II and I) up to the snowy West Summit P.4009 and the Rimpfischsattel beyond (3985m, 4 hrs from Flue). This point can also be reached from the Britannia Hut (or the Täsch Hut) via the Allalinpass then taking a line across the slopes below the North-West Face (5 hrs).

From P.4009 head east up an icy snow slope and into a couloir between two rock ribs (best taken close to the right) flanking rocks. After about 50m of climbing quit the tempting direct line which leads to a tiring thrash and traverse left (north) over ledges and a recess to a notch on the West Ridge of the fore-summit. Climb directly up the stepped ridge edge on good firm holds using the right flank at one point on a slab (II+), to gain the fore-summit. Go down into the notch beyond, then scramble up the exposed ridge to the main summit (1-2 hrs from the Rimpfischsattel).

View: A good vantage point for both the mighty Zermatt and Saas panoramas. To the north is the Mischabel group and Allalinhorn, to the east, the very white Strahlhorn, to the south the Monte Rosa massif, with particularly good views of the north-west slope of the Nordend and the ice-cliffs of the North-West Face of the Liskamm, to the south-west are the Breithorn and the Matterhorn and to the north-west the Weisshorn.

Adjacent peaks: The **West Summit P.4009** is traversed on ascent. The big **North Ridge gendarme P.4108** is most easily climbed from the Allalinpass on an ascent of the North Ridge.

Other worthwhile routes: *North Ridge* (AD, pitches of III, the gendarme by the south edge direct is IV, from the Allalinpass 4-5 hrs).
East Face (D, pitches of IV, mostly III, mixed; from the Adlerpass 3-4 hrs; the best route if combining this mountain with an ascent the Strahlhorn).
North-West Face (small but fine, 300mH, ice to 55°).

Guidebook: Pennine Alps East (The Alpine Club, 1975).

Strahlhorn, 4190m

From the Moro Pass and the Ofen valley, the East Face is conspicuous as a mighty rock triangle, but the ordinary route over the glacier-covered north side is a snow plod. No wonder that here the thought of a pair of floating skis occurs even to moderate skiers (even if ski ascents right to the top are usual only in very good conditions). The first ascent was made in 1854 in the 'Golden Age' of alpinism by E.J. Grenville and Christopher Smyth, led by Franz Joseph Andenmatten and Ulrich Lauener.

The ascent from the west to the Adlerpass is, in winter, part of the last big stage of the Haute Route. In the summer, however, it has recently developed a reputation for its increasingly chaotic crevasse systems.

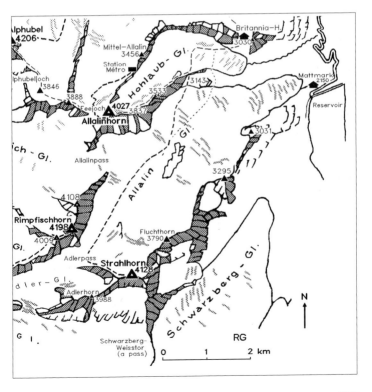

Difficulties: PD. Technically a pure plod. In mist, if the track is lost, route-finding is difficult. This is because the twists and turns needed to avoid the ice-falls on the Allalin Glacier prevent a straight compass bearing to the foot of the South-East Face of the Rimpfischhorn.

Effort: The hut climb utilizing the cableway to the Felskinn takes about 30 mins, and the summit climb is 1250mH (4-5 hrs).

Dangers: Extensive glacier work with miscellaneous well-camouflaged trap-doors.

Pleasures: Only really enjoyable on skis.

Maps: LKS 1348 Zermatt and LKS 1328 Randa, also LKS 5006 Matterhorn-Mischabel.

Hut climb: To the Britannia Hut, see Allalinhorn; to Flue, see Rimpfischhorn.

Summit route via the Adler Pass and the West Ridge: From the Britannia Hut head west on the path down the slope to the Hohlaub Glacier. Cross this at about 3000m to the foot of the Hohlaubgrat descending from the Allalinhorn (P.3143). Now on the Allalin Glacier, ascend parallel to the faces breaking off south-eastwards from the Hohlaubgrat. Cross the flatter glacier bottom under the junction of the ice stream descending from the Allalinpass and then pass under the east walls of the Rimpfischhorn (crevasses!) to gain the Adler Pass (3789m, from Flue 4 hrs). Continue on the initially defined, then broader, North-West Ridge over P.3957 and P.4128 to the summit.

Adjacent peaks: Points **P.4128** and **P.4143** are only really ridge upswings and cannot really be described as tops.

Other worthwhile routes: *North-East Ridge* (AD, possibly combined with the Fluchthorn; snow climb, on the summit block rock to II, 1250 or 1330mH, 4-5 hrs from Britannia Hut).

West-South-West Ridge (AD, in summer mostly problematical on the Adler Glacier, best combined with the Adlerhorn – 3988m; 1600mH, 6 hrs from Gasthaus Flue).

South Face (AD+, in part II, mostly mixed, and snow, from the Schwarzberg-Weisstor over rock face, snow terrace and summit wall. Conveniently reached from the Sella Hut over Neues Weisstor, 1200mH, 5 hrs, alternatively from the Gasthaus Flue. 1600mH, 6-7 hrs).

Guidebook: Pennine Alps East (The Alpine Club, 1975).

These mountains between the Matter valley and Val d'Hérens are in a more natural state than those of the more popular peaks to the east. No mountain railways or cableways disfigure the slopes. No quick weekend traffic overruns the mountain range. Here the huts are high and the paths long. The mountains are free from obtrusive ski villages marring their lower slopes.

Bishorn, 4153m

The Bishorn is situated to the north of the Weisshorn and, with a drop of only 120m between them is not very independent. Even though it is one of the less exacting 4000ers on the climb above the hut, it is still quite a demanding peak as the entire approach must still be done without transport and the valley is far below. The summit is often visited in both winter and summer, thanks to the modest difficulties of its North-West Face. It was probably climbed for the first time in 1884 by Joseph Imboden and J.M. Chanton with G.S. Barnes and R. Chessyre-Walker.

Difficulties: F. A snow plod, with a little easy climbing on the summit ridge (I).

Effort: The hut climb is a hard 1580mH (5 hrs), summit ascent 900mH (2-3 hrs, a departure at 5 or 6 a.m. suffices).

Dangers: The glaciers always have crevasses. On ascent to the summit ridge look out for cornices above the North-East Face.

Pleasures: The singular view from the summit ridge of the nearby show-piece, the Weisshorn.

Maps: LKS 1327 Evolène and LKS 1328 Randa, also LKS 5006 Matterhorn-Mischabel.

Travel: By rail through the Rhône valley to Sierre, from there by bus or car 28km through the Val D'Anniviers to Zinal (1680m, a tourist resort with moderate development and refreshingly original surroundings, campsite).

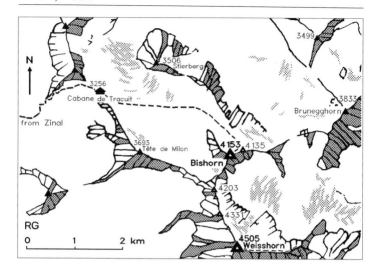

Hut climb: From the southern end of the town, before reaching the campsite at the hamlet of Les Doberts, head east on a prominent zig-zag track up to Alpe Tracuit (Chiesso, 2061m). Continue in wide bends above, then turn southwards to work up into the valley of the Torrent du Barmé and then north-east to Alm Combautanna (2578m). Continue over sparser slopes to the *Tracuit Hut* by the Col Tracuit just before reaching the Turtmann Glacier (3256m, SAC Chaussy, 140 B, managed from mid-June to mid-September, Tel. 027-65 15 00).

Summit route by the North-West Face: From the hut take an easterly line over the Turtmann Glacier to its eastern arm, keeping well away from the drop to its north-east (potential cornices). Go steadily up the slope of the North-West Face to the notch between the two summits and turn right and ascend the ridge, often corniced, to the highest point.

View: To the south the nearby Weisshorn dominates, to the east is the Mischabel group and to the north the Bernese Oberland.

Adjacent peaks: The prominent east summit – **Pointe Burnaby (4135m).**

Other worthwhile routes: *North-East Face* (TD, a fine ice face with passages of 70°-90° 650mH, 4-6 hrs from the bergschrund).

South-West Ridge from the Weisshornjoch (PD, II, 3 hrs).

Guidebook: Pennine Alps Central (The Alpine Club, 1975).

Weisshorn, 4505m

A magnificent pyramid, from the north-east a white triangle, from the south-east and south-west rocky with snow couloirs, but after new snow-fall the whole mountain looks icily white. It has three evocative knife-edged ridges at the meeting of the steep faces, giving it all the appearance of the ideal peak. The Weisshorn doesn't have quite the same arresting presence as the Matterhorn as it does not stand so strategically above a big valley town. But it is still finely sculpted, unfolding its full splendour only to those who take the trouble to visit its heights.

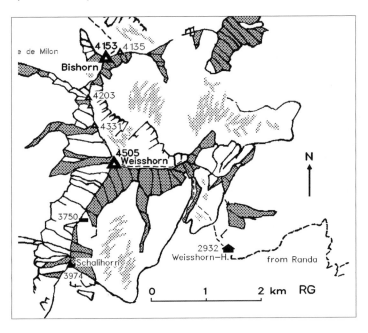

The first ascent was made in 1861 by John Tyndall (whose first attempts on the Matterhorn are commemorated in the naming of one of its ridge pinnacles) with the aid of the guides J.J. Bennen and U. Wenger on today's ordinary route from Randa by the East Ridge. The South Ridge, or Schalligrat, the most exacting of the three, was overcome in 1895 by Joseph Biner and Ambros Imboden with Edward Broome, and three years later, in 1898 the entire North Ridge was traversed by H. Biehly and

H. Burgener. The Younggrat to the Grand Gendarme of the North Ridge was climbed in 1900 by the Alpine poet Geoffrey Winthrop Young with the Zinal guides Louis and Benoit Theytaz (who later developed it into a fixed rope route with iron stakes, but this has now been removed). Young, accompanied by V.J.E. Ryan, Josef and Gabriel Lochmatter and Josef Knubel also climbed the South Face taking a mighty diagonal directly to the summit. The North-East Face, with its dangerous séracs, fell to Young and Knubel in 1909, accompanied by the American climber, Oliver Perry-Smith, famous for his exploits on Saxony sandstone.

In contrast to many of the other high Alpine peaks, not only has the ordinary route remained just as difficult as on its original ascent, but also the full valley approach must still be climbed, making this one of the most demanding Alpine summits in terms of the overall effort required.

Difficulties: AD. Rock-climbing with pitches of III, but mostly II and I and snow ridge to 45°.

Effort: A wretched 1500mH hut climb (5 hrs) and then a 1600mH summit climb (6-7 hrs) on which it is advised not to start too early on account of route-finding problems on the approach to P.3916.

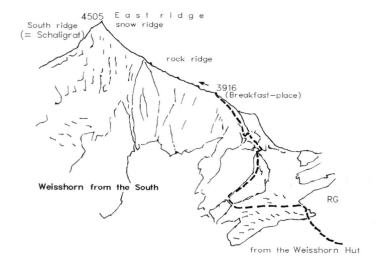

Weisshorn from the South

Weisshorn and Bishorn (right) from the east.

Dangers: On the glacier take the customary crevasse precautions and on the ridge beware of cornices. A helmet is advisable as there is some stone-fall danger from other parties, especially below Frühstücksplatz (breakfast site) on both ascent and descent. On that section try to avoid the gullies and keep to the rock ribs.

Pleasures: A mountain which enjoys a reputation as one of the most beautiful in the Alps (or indeed the world) situated in an unspoilt and wild part of the range.

Maps: LKS 1328 Randa, also LKS 5006 Matterhorn-Mischabel.

Travel: By rail or car from Visp in the Rhône valley 23km to *Randa* (1408m; small place with moderate tourist traffic, no mountain railways).

Hut climb: From Randa railway station go along the valley road 200m northwards to the bridge over the stream and up to the Eien-Hütten [huts]. Above these go up the valley slope heading south-west through light woodland in numerous zig-zags to shortly before the Rotiböden Hut (1970m). Now go right and ascend to the Jatz-Alpe (c.2280m). The path goes west-south-west over grass slopes, crossing two streams and climbing obliquely over further slopes to the *Weisshorn Hut* (2932m, SAC Basel, 40 B, managed from mid-July to mid-September, Tel. 028-67 12 62).

Summit Route by the East Ridge: Head north-west on a path leading to the most easterly basin of the Schali Glacier. Traverse this obliquely leftwards (west) to a rock rib, which descends from the East Ridge. To gain the rib climb the prominent couloir (just right of P.3145), starting on the right but soon moving to the rocks on the left to gain the top of the rib. Climb the snow slopes on the left beside the rib to the rock barrier at its upper end. At this point move right, over exposed snow and slabs (II, harder if bare) to gain a snow or debris shoulder. (Daylight is advisable for the next section.) Climb a short snow and debris ridge to a rock wall which is taken straight up for a few metres before following a ledge leading downwards to the left to a terrace with prominent cairn. From here, zig-zag several hundred metres up the edge of a rubble spur up to the lower rocky part of the East Ridge (P.3916, Frühstücksplatz, 3 hrs from hut).

Climb the airy ridge with numerous steps and gendarmes. Most of them are climbed direct, but on the difficult Lochmatter Tower, just above the Frühstücksplatz, iron posts assist a traverse on the left (south). The uppermost tower is traversed on the right (one hour from P.3916). Beyond this the upper snow ridge is reached by a knife-edged snow arête (sometimes corniced). Continue up the steep, featureless snow ridge (small bergschrund) to rocks preceeding the summit.

View: The Mischabel group can be seen to the east over the Matter valley, to the south are the summits at the head of the Zermatt valley and to the south-west is the Dent Blanche.

Adjacent peaks: The uppermost **East Ridge Gendarme (P.4178)** is usually turned during the ascent. On the North Ridge the **Grand Gendarme (P.4331)** stands out distinctly, 50 metres above the col. The remaining North Ridge elevations **P.4362, P.4203** and **P4108** are by comparison only modest.

Other worthwhile routes: *North Ridge* (AD+, III+, mixed, snow 45°, 450mH from Weisshornjoch, 8 hrs from Tracuit Hut).

Younggrat (D, elegant rock-climbing to IV, should be dry, old iron pegs from a long-dismantled climbing 'path' are useful as belays, 6-8 hrs from Cabane d'Ar Pitetta).

South Ridge or Schaligrat (D, elegant rock-climbing to IV, 750mH from the Schali Bivouac, with adventurous approaches to this; from there 5-7 hrs to the summit).

North-East Rib (D, a classic ice route, 7-10 hrs).

Guidebook: Pennine Alps Central (The Alpine Club, 1975).

Zinalrothorn, 4221m

This is a very slim peak of firm gneiss and that gives it a particularly exciting character. When Leslie Stephen and F. Crauford Grove let themselves be led up by Jakob and Melchior Anderegg on the first ascent in 1864, this was over the pinnacled and very exposed North Ridge. Today's ordinary route on the Zinalrothorn (often abbreviated to 'Rothorn') takes in the South-East Ridge and the Gabel notch. The upper part of the South-West Ridge was climbed first in 1872 by Alexander Burgener, Ferdinand Imseng and Franz Andermatten with Clinton T. Dent and G.A. Passingham. The distinctly more difficult South-West Ridge integral (Rothorngrat) is acclaimed as an outstanding route. That was climbed by C.R. Gross with the guide R. Taugwalder in 1901. In 1909 Geoffrey Winthrop Young with his trusty guides Knubel and Marcus and his compatriot C.D. Robertson ventured on the right-hand part of the East Face and climbed it to the North Ridge below the Sphinx. The steep, direct South-East Ridge (Kanzelgrat) was overcome in three stages during five years beginning in 1928, by E.R. Blanchet and Kaspar Mooser using a variety of aids. The breathtakingly precipitous and loose East Face fell to André Roch, Robert Gréloz and Ruedi Schmidt in 1945.

Like other peaks in the vicinity, not one metre of this noble mountain is made easier by mountain railways or cableways so that its full challenge is preserved.

Difficulties: AD–. In part exposed rock-climbing to III–, mostly II and I. When icy or in new snow, these sections soon become impassable for climbers of average ability.

Effort: Hut climb 1700mH (5 hrs), summit climb 1050mH (4-5 hrs).

Dangers: On the lower part of the ridge, beware of cornices. In the couloir and on the summit ridge there are often tricky iced-up sections.

Pleasures: Enjoyable climbing, particularly on the spectacular summit ridge.

Maps: LKS 1327 Evolène, LKS 1348 Zermatt, LKS 1328 Randa, also LKS 5006 Matterhorn-Mischabel.

Travel: To *Zermatt*, see Dufourspitze/Monte Rosa (page 124).

Hut climb: From Zermatt railway station walk about five minutes through the town and then ascend westwards north of the Triftbach. Subsequently, move to the south of the stream and go up the side of the Triftschlucht (steep) to the Gasthaus Edelweiss (1961m, shown on the LKS map as 'Alterhaupt'). Continue across the slope of the picturesque gorge and cross back to the north bank, to the venerable Trifthotel (2337m). Climb on a broad track over a pasture bottom and slopes to the Vieliboden and to the shallow but picturesque pool of the Triftsee (2579m). After that, ascend the northern moraine of the Trift Glacier in several dozen bends and then a short section of snow climbing leads to the *Rothorn Hut* which is in front of the rock spur Eseltschuggen, an outlier of the Zinalrothorn's South-East Ridge (3178m, SAC Ober-Aargau, 104 B, managed from the end of June to mid-September, Tel. 028-67 20 43).

Summit climb by the South-East Ridge: From the hut head north along the western side of the Rothorn Glacier until below a snow break splitting the rock wall on the left. Turn and ascend this to the foot of a rock step which is climbed by a chimney/gully starting from the lowest point. From the top of the step continue up mixed ground then snow slopes to gain the ridge (breakfast place). Head north along the ridge, first up rock (trending left) and then by a snow ridge to reach a point just west of P.3786 where a subsidiary ridge comes in from the east.

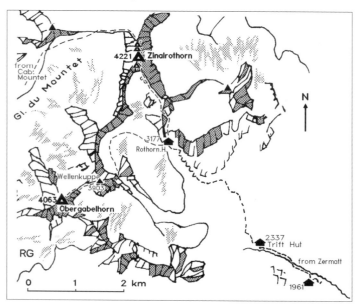

Zinalrothorn from the east (from the Matter valley south of Randa).
On the left is the South-East Ridge leading to the summit block, on the right the North Ridge.

Now heading north-west, move up the narrowing ridge, first over rock, then over snow (cornices) to P.3912. At this point, below the final steep section of the Kanzelgrat, climb two steep rock steps, then traverse left, first into a couloir and then up and across rocks and snow beds on the South Face to gain a snow couloir on the upper part of the face below the Gabel notch. Climb the bed of the couloir or (if there is stone-fall danger from parties above) on the bordering rocks on the left (II+) up to the prominent Gabel notch of the South-West Ridge by a two-headed gendarme (3 hrs from the hut).

Move directly up the ridge for about 50m to a stance at the foot of a steep rise. Here, descend left through a cleft to the Biner Slab, which is often iced up. Climb this by a slanting crack (peg), or turn it on the west side, and then climb a rock rib (III−) to regain the ridge (or on the left if the rib is iced up). Make an exposed traverse of a gendarme on the left (west) to the fore-summit ('Kanzel'). Turn this on the right (above the very impressive East Face) on a broad ledge and over a last piece of ridge to the highest point (1-2 hrs from the Gabel).

View: The summit is high enough to give an extensive panorama, but nevertheless low enough to make several of the neighbouring peaks appear huge. To the north the Weisshorn dominates, towering up behind the Schalihorn. To the west the extensive Mountet Glacier basin of the Zinal Glacier is dominated by the Dent Blanche and the Grand Cornier. To the south-west, continuing the ridge, are the Trifthorn and Wellenkuppe and behind them the Obergabelhorn. To the south beyond the Wellenkuppe, the Matterhorn looks particularly splendid from this angle, and east of that, closing the Zermatt valley are the Breithorn, Liskamm and Monte Rosa. Finally, to the east, are Rimpfischhorn, Alphubel and the Mischabel group.

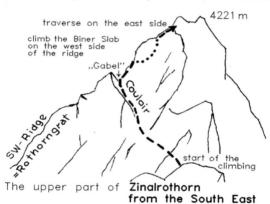

The upper part of **Zinalrothorn from the South East**

Adjacent peaks: On the South-West Ridge, the fore-summit or **Kanzel** is **c.4200m** and the prominent fork-shaped **gendarme** above the Gabel is **c.4100m**. On the North Ridge there is the striking **Bosse (c.4150m)** and the narrow pinnacle edge of the **Sphinx (c.4100m)** and rather lower down the prominent shoulder of the **Epaule (P.4017)** on a kink in the ridge. These points are so lacking in independence that, with the exception of the Epaule, they have never been exactly measured.

Other worthwhile routes: *North Ridge* (AD, III+ and II, 1400mH, 5 hrs from Mountet Hut).

South-West Ridge or *Rothorngrat* (D, IV and III+, one of the finest ridge climbs in the Alps with excellent rock and a fine position, 370mH, 3-4 hrs from Ober-Rotjoch, 1100mH, 7 hrs from Rothorn Hut).

Kanzelgrat (TD–, V and IV+, which provides a more difficult and direct finish to the ordinary route that avoids both the unpleasant couloir and the Biner Slab, 4-5 hrs from starting climb).

East Face Direct (TD, to V+, 8 hrs from foot of face).

Guidebook: Pennine Alps Central (The Alpine Club, 1975).

Obergabelhorn, 4063m

This is a symmetrical, four-sided pyramid, with a North-East Face bristling with ice and a sunny South Face. In a ranking of the most beautiful mountains in the Alps, there are many people who set this peak absolutely at the top, ahead of the Weisshorn and Matterhorn.

The first ascent was carried out in 1865 by Jakob Anderegg with A.W. Moore and Horace Walker from the east from the Gabelhorn Glacier. Only a day later, Peter Taugwalder and Josef Vianin reached the summit by the North-North-West Ridge (Coeurgrat) with Lord Francis Douglas, shortly before his death on the Matterhorn. The noted West-South-West Ridge (Arbengrat) fell in 1874 to H. Seymour Hoare and E. Hulton with Johann von Bergen, J. Moser and Peter Rubi. The unjustly neglected South-East Ridge (Gabelhorngrat) was climbed in 1877 by Edward Davidson and J.W. Hartley with Johann Jaun and Peter Rubi. Today's ordinary route by the North-East Ridge from the Wellenkuppe was first done in 1890 by L. Norman-Neruda with the Engadine guide Christian Klucker. This ascent first became popular in 1918, after the great gendarme had been rendered harmless with a fixed rope. The pleasant climbing up the South Face was first discovered by Daniel Maquignaz with his client J.P. Farrar in 1892. The first ascent of the graceful ice veil of the North Face was made by the Austrians Hans Kiener and Rudolf Schwarzgruber in 1930.

Difficulties: AD. Rock-climbing on the Wellenkuppe to II+, on the traverse to the Obergabelhorn there are some sections of III (if using the fixed rope on the Kluckerturm), but mostly it is II and I, mixed, and a snow ridge with ice slopes up to 50°. The difficulty varies considerably with the state of the track and whether steps have been cut.
Effort: Hut climb 1700mH (5 hrs), summit climb 850mH (5-6 hrs).
Dangers: Typical glacier problems on the approach to the Wellenkuppe and cornices on the connecting ridge to the Obergabelhorn.
Pleasures: An intricate ascent of a beautiful Alpine peak.

Maps, sketches, travel, hut climb: See Zinalrothorn.
Summit climb by the North-East Ridge: From the Rothorn Hut head north-west and make a wide left arc under the uppermost

ice-fall of the Trift Glacier (crevasses!) and rising up under the Trifthorn gain access to a snow shoulder on the East-North-East Ridge of the Wellenkuppe (c.3650m). Turn the first ridge rise on the left (south) between rock and a snow patch and after crossing a small couloir on less difficult rocks go up to the ridge. Follow this for about 100 metres to a rocky crest which can be turned on the left on snow. After that, continue on the slabby ridge over a last rise to the summit of the **Wellenkuppe** (3903m).

Head west to a saddle on the initially broad but soon narrowing, snow ridge (cornices) to the foot of the Grand Gendarme (Kluckerturm). Climb some (mostly) icy slabs and ribs (III, old fixed stanchions) to the fixed cable and, with its help, go strenuously up the remaining 20m to the top of the gendarme (or free on the left IV+). Beyond the gendarme, on the steep face of the snow ridge, heavily corniced on the left (south) side, cross first into a small saddle then go steeply up to the summit ridge to the rocky summit block, keeping just right of the ridge edge throughout on snowy rock with good holds.

View: To the south are the Matterhorn and Dent d'Hérens in all their majesty, to the west the equally splendid Dent Blanche and to the north-east is the Zinalrothorn. All these peaks, because of their greater height, are especially impressive to look at.

Adjacent peaks: The Grand Gendarme (P.3870) on the East Ridge.

Other worthwhile routes: *West-South-West Ridge or Arbengrat* (AD, to III+, 1200mH, 6 hrs from the Mountet Hut. This is particularly useful as a descent route to complete a traverse, but take care to descend to the Arben valley from the correct point above the Arbenjoch where the descent is not pleasant. Alternatively cross Mont Durand and go down via the Schönbiel Hut).

North-North-West Ridge or Coeurgrat (AD, III, mixed, and ice to 50°, 6 hrs from the Mountet Hut, highly praised).

South-East Ridge or Gabelhorngrat (AD+, 850mH, 4 hrs from the Arben Bivouac Hut).

South Face (AD, IV and III, on firm gneiss, 850mH, 6 hrs from the Arben Bivouac Hut. Note: In 1974 a British party encountered loose rock on this face with fatal consequences.)

North Face (TD−, ice or snow to 55°, finally over steeper mixed ground, and with difficulty fluctuating considerably, 1250mH from the Mountet Hut, 500mH from start of climb).

Guidebook: Pennine Alps Central (The Alpine Club, 1975).

Dent Blanche, 4356m

A mighty, free-standing, slightly tilted, gneiss pyramid. The bold, exposed and unashamedly long ridges are set exactly on the four points of the compass. Between them, unfriendly, broken faces fall away.

The first ascent was made in 1862 by Jean-Baptiste Croz and Johann Kronig with Thomas Stuart Kennedy and William Wigram. They took the South Ridge, which, although very demanding is still used as the ordinary route, though it is easier these days because of a very high hut. The beautiful East Ridge or Viereselsgrat, which has no such amenity, was first climbed in 1882 by Ulrich Almer and A. Pollinger with J. Stafford Anderson and G.P. Baker. The technically more difficult Ferpècle Ridge fell in 1889 to A. Pollinger with his client W. Gröbli. The North Face first climbed in 1930 by K. Schneider and F. Singer and straightened in 1966 by Michel and Yvette Vaucher is regarded as one of the fiercest undertakings in the Pennine Alps.

Difficulties: AD. Rock to III, mixed, on snow to 35°.
Effort: The hut climb involves a strenuous approach of 1700mH (5-7 hrs), leaving a summit climb of 850mH (3-6 hrs).
Dangers: On the ridge there can be big cornices and the whole thing is exposed to the wind, which can greatly complicate the long stretches of tricky climbing. In iced up conditions (not infrequent) they become quite difficult.
Pleasures: A regal summit set in a stately and isolated position.

Maps: LKS 1327 Evolène and LKS 1347 Matterhorn, also LKS 5006 Matterhorn-Mischabel.
Travel: By rail to Sion in the Rhône valley, from there 33km by post bus to *Les Haudères* (1450m, a refreshingly quiet tourist resort, also campsite). Another 7km by car via La Forclaz and Salay to the Ferpècle car-park (beyond Salay, before bridge).
Hut climb: Continue up the road to the water works. Before reaching the stream, go left through the wood and climb steadily on good path south-eastwards over pasture slopes to Alpe Bricola (2415m; original old stone huts and a closed hotel building. Move on in the same direction over sparser terrain above the Ferpècle glacier. Finally work up south-east onto the northern moraine of the Manzettes Glacier which descends

from the west side of the Dent Blanche. Traverse laboriously south across the moraines and the glacier tongue, to gain the southern edge, working up over snow parallel to the slabs and block ridge of the Roc Noir. Further up, still heading in the same direction, climb over an ice top to the *Dent Blanche Hut* placed at the foot of a rock ridge (Roussier Hut, 3507m, SAC Jaman, 40 B, managed from mid-July to the beginning of September, Tel.).

Summit climb by the South Ridge/Wandfluegrat: Go up the rocky ridge immediately behind the hut and then up an ice slope to the wide saddle of the Wandfluelucke (3703m). Continue to the north over easy block ridge to the snow top of P.3907. The increasingly rugged ridge continues up to the foot of the prominent Grand Gendarme. Either climb directly (IV) or pass it by an oblique line to the left (west) over slabs for about 50m and then by a sort of gully to the notch right of a prominent lateral pinnacle. From this notch take a shallow, icy couloir, III, 3 iron posts for belays and abseiling) steeply up into the notch behind the Grand Gendarme. The next towers can be crossed directly, but it is still easier to turn the second one on the right (east) and the third one on the left (west) over often icy slabs. Before reaching the last tower traverse 20m to the left and climb a

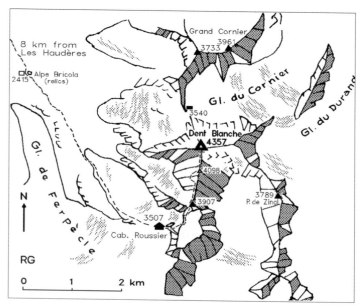

118

Dent Blanche from the west (from the Aiguille de la Tsa). South Ridge on the right.

two-metre wall following a (usually icy) groove up to the ridge again. After that continue on the less difficult snow ridge (occasional cornices) to the summit cross.

View: Fantastic panorama from Mont Blanc and Grand Combin to Monte Rosa, Weisshorn and Mischabel group. Special attractions are the somewhat unusual but no less impressive views of the Matterhorn and the Dent d'Hérens North Face.

Adjacent peaks: The non-independent but prominent Grand Gendarme (4098m) on the South Ridge is quickly reached from the narrow col above by difficult climbing.

Other worthwhile routes: *East Ridge or Viereselsgrat* (D, III+ and III, mixed, serious, long, delicate and exposed yet still popular, 1500mH, 11-15 hrs from the Mountet Hut).
West Ridge or Ferpècle Ridge (D+, rock-climbing to IV+, IV and III, mixed 850mH, 7hrs. from start of climb).
North Ridge (TD+, rock to V+, mixed, fierce, dangerous, 950mH, 12-15 hrs from the foot of the face).

Guidebook: Pennine Alps Central (The Alpine Club, 1975).

The watershed, likewise the frontier, runs along the main crest of the Alps between Switzerland and Italy. Here the highest summits lie impressively strung in a row: to the east the broad massif of Monte Rosa, after that the narrower and almost rectilinear middle section and finally, far removed, to the west, the Grand Combin.

Nordend, 4609m

As part of the Monte Rosa massif, the third highest alpine summit possesses, with a drop to the col height of only 94 metres, only limited independence. It has, nevertheless, an independent long-distance approach and is also inconvenient to combine with the ascent of the main summit. Above all, aspirants frequently have to find the route on the glacier themselves, for it is not often done and the wind quickly drifts over the track.

Several parties reached the Silbersattel but were rebuffed on the ridge by the then apparently considerable bergschrunds, and it was not until the 1861 that the first ascent was made by E.N. and T.F. Buxton and J.J. Cowell with the French guide Michel Payot and the Swiss guide Binder. The first ascent from the Jägerhorn direction using the North-East Ridge (Cresta di Santa Catarina) was made in 1906 by Franz and Josef Lochmatter with V.J.E. Ryan. This was, at that time, an outstanding undertaking made without any aid from pitons, a factor that should sober anyone making a modern ascent of this fine and remote route.

Difficulties: PD. A glacier climb which offers variable difficulties and is often without track! On the summit block there are pitches of II and I.

Effort: Hut climb from the Gornergrat railway 300mH descent and 250mH ascent (2 hrs, from Zermatt on foot 4-5 hrs, summit climb 1820mH, 6-7 hrs).

Dangers: The firmness of the crevasse bridges in the upper part is a factor, as they have been untested. Anyone who doesn't respect the cornices that overhang the enormous East Face on the summit ridge can fall around two-and-a-half thousand metres. The time schedule should allow the descent of the glacier to be completed not later than 1 p.m!

Pleasures: A beautiful, seldom visited summit that provides a full palette of route-finding difficulties, with the corresponding satisfactions of pioneering exploration.

Maps, travel, hut climbs: See Dufourspitze.

Summit climb: From the Monte Rosa Hut (2795m) as for ordinary route to the Dufourspitze as far as the hollow before the slope of the 'Satteltole' (c.4100m). Now leave the generally tracked route and continue left (east) into the glacier basin between Nordend on the left and Dufourspitze on the right, through a system of big snow crevasses and over a bergschrund up to the Silbersattel (4515m, which is also the finishing point for the main routes up Monte Rosa's enormous East Face).

Ascend on the west side of the corniced South Ridge, traversing a small ridge hump (P.4542) and finally climbing rocks (II and I) to the summit.

View: The curved course of the whole summit ridge allows a stupendous view to the south-east down the highest ice face in the Alps. The panorama to the south is somewhat restricted by the nearby Dufourspitze, though still impressive.

Adjacent peaks: P.4542 on the South Ridge, traversed during the ascent.

Other worthwhile routes: *North-West Buttress* (AD, II, mixed, snow to 40° from the Monte Rosa Glacier north of P.3696, snow and a reddish rock rib to P.4071, 1800mH from the hut, and 1000mH from start of climb (1800mH from hut), from there 7-8 hrs to summit).

Morshead Spur (AD, pitches of IV, otherwise II and mixed, from P.4200 at the foot of the West Face go direct to the north-west snow slope; 2-3 hrs from start of climb).

North-East Ridge or Cresta di Santa Catarina (TD–, IV with one section of V, mostly mixed, 700mH from the Città di Gallarate Bivouac on the Jägerhorn, from there a difficult 450mH, 5-7 hrs from the bivouac to the summit, large-scale classic ascent).

East Face, Brioschi Route (D+, IV and III and ice to 60°, 2300mH, from the Marinelli Hut 1580mH, from there 9-12 hrs, a marvellous climb up a wild and remote ice face).

Traverse to Dufourspitze (AD, pitches of III, mixed, over the Grenzgipfel and summit ridge, 2 hrs from the Silbersattel.

Guidebook: Pennine Alps Central (The Alpine Club, 1975).

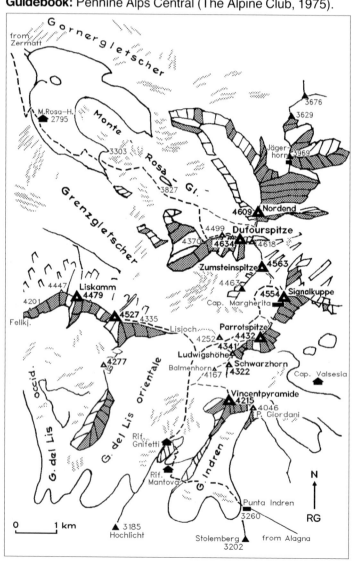

Dufourspitze, 4634m

Monte Rosa is the most enormous mountain massif in the Alps – that Mont Blanc rises higher in the sky is thanks only to the extremely hard granite of which it is composed. In terms of mountain mass (ground above 4000m), however, it is easily beaten by Monte Rosa and its satellites.

The ascent of the ordinary route on the Dufourspitze is also considerably more demanding than Mont Blanc's ordinary route, because on the Dufourspitze Ridge the main difficulties occur on the summit ridge. The first ascent was made in 1855 by a considerable caravan, paid for by Charles Hudson (who fell on descent from the Matterhorn ten years later), John Birkbeck, E.J. Stephenson and J.G. and C. Smythe, the track being opened up for them by the guides J. and M. Zumtaugwald from Zermatt and Ulrich Lauener from Lauterbrunnen. The summit was named after the publisher of the first precise Swiss map. The classic route up the 2500m East Face, which Erich Vanis has compared with a Himalayan face, was opened up as early as 1872 by the international party comprising Englishmen Richard and William Pendlebury and Charles Taylor with the Swiss Ferdinand Imseng, the Austrian Gabriel Spechtenhauser and the Italian Giovanni Oberto.

Difficulties: PD. A long glacier-plod as a prelude to summit ridge climbing to II+, mostly I, mixed, on exposed rock, rounded by crampon scratches, with ice to 40°.

Effort: To the hut from the Gornergrat railway, 300mH descent, 250mH ascent (2 hrs, if walking from Zermatt an additional 1220mH taking in total 5-6 hrs), summit climb 1880mH (5-7 hrs).

Dangers: On the glacier there is normally a broad trail, but in mist and with the track drifted over there can be serious route-finding difficulties with corresponding crevasse dangers. Initially, on the summit ridge, there are few natural belay possibilities, but on the harder summit block there are useful pinnacles and spikes. On the summit ridge especially, good windproof clothing is often of decisive importance. The long descent over the glacier should be completed by about 1 p.m., before the snow becomes bad and the crevasse bridges soften.

Pleasures: A summit that must be 'toiled for' and whose ascent thus provides especially deep satisfaction. In addition, there is a fantastic panorama.

Maps: LKS 1348 Zermatt; LKS 5006 Matterhorn-Mischabel.

Travel: By rail via Visp/Rhône valley-Stalden-Täsch up the Matter valley to *Zermatt* (1606m, full of tradition, an exclusive tourist resort with all the trimmings, including a Youth Hostel, a Naturfreundeheim or Friends of Nature Hostel and an alpine museum with all sorts of ghoulish objects). No cars are allowed – these must be left in a big car-park in Täsch and the journey completed by train.

Hut climb: From the Rotenboden station (2815m) of the Gornergrat railway take the track south past the Riffelsee and Riffelhorn and into a hollow, then down a gradually descending path to the dry Gorner Glacier. Traverse the bare ice (markers), crossing the block wall of the central moraine then up by the lightly crevassed ice of the adjoining Grenz Glacier to the polished rocks of the eastern glacier bank. Before reaching a crevasse system, move on to the rocks and climb up a good path in long zig-zags to the bank moraine and the *Monte Rosa Hut* (2795m, SAC, 128 B, managed from mid-March to mid-September, Tel. 028-67 21 15).

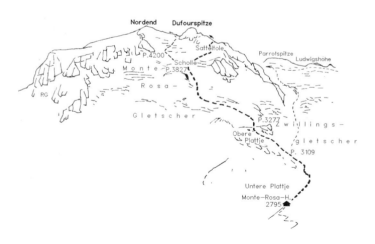

Nordend from the summit of the Dufourspitze.

Summit route by the East Ridge: From the hut take the lateral moraine for a spell, then follow cairns over the polished rocks and the debris of the Unteren Plattje and on up a steep step to the Obere Plattje (3200m).

Move up onto the Monte Rosa Glacier, soon trending left through a crevasse system and then up by the glacier trough keeping south of the straggling rock island of P.3827. Climbing steeply up the 'Scholle' to reach the foot of the broad slope of the 'Satteltole'. Head up this to a final steep section leading to Sattel at P.4359 on the West Ridge of the Dufourspitze.

Now work east along the ridge, at first on an icy knife-edge, then over broken rock to the rocky ridge hump (P.4499). On the other side, descend a little and continue up a snow slope and rock to the fore-summit. A rocky ridge with pinnacles and blocks leads down into a notch and steeply up cracks and steps, with good holds scratched by many crampons, in the final part keeping left of the ridge edge to eventually pull onto the summit.

View: Lower summits all around, but nearby there is a whole collection of satellites, especially on the Pennine frontier crest running from the Signalkuppe westwards to the Liskamm. The glacier scenery is particularly impressive with the scale of the Grenz and Monte Rosa Glaciers – emphasised from this vantage. To the west the Matterhorn and Weisshorn groups stand in sharp profile.

Adjacent peaks: The **Grenzgipfel P.4618**, the easterly corner point of the summit ridge 150m away is occasionally even done as an independent summit (and despite its closeness still offers problems). In between there is another ridge tower, **Gratturm, c.4630m**. These two elevations can be climbed on the traverse of the ridge to the Zumsteinspitze and Signalkuppe. On the West Ridge, besides the **fore-summit (c.4600m)**, about 60m away from the highest point, the **Upper West Ridge Summit P.4499** and, west of the saddle, the **Lower West Ridge Summit (c.4380m)** can be distinguished. The two first named are traversed on the ordinary route, the last named is quickly reached from the saddle P.4359.

Other worthwhile routes: *Descent over the frontier summit and Zumsteinspitze to the Signalkuppe* (AD, III and II, 3 hrs to Marghérita Hut).

Traverse from the Silbersattel along the frontier summit to the Dufourspitze (AD, III and II, mixed, often made harder by ice and snow, 2 hrs to the main summit).

Traverse from the Zumsteinspitze along the frontier summit to the Dufourspitze (AD, III and II, mixed, 2-3 hrs).

South Rib or Cresta Rey (AD, III- and II, an ideal line, steep rock, dries quickly, long glacier approach, then 400mH from start of climb, 3 hrs).

East Face or Marinelli Couloir (D+, at 2400mH the mightiest ice face in the Alps, around 50°-55°, by direct exit over the rock rib to the Grenzgipfel also climbing to III+, very menaced by falling ice, especially in mild weather, 9-12 hrs from the Marinelli Hut).

Guidebook: Pennine Alps Central (The Alpine Club, 1975).

Zumsteinspitze, 4563m

This rock pyramid is only a blip between Dufourspitze and Signalkuppe – but in what a situation! Seen from the north-east, it crowns the mighty East Face of Monte Rosa and from the west it stands at the source of the wild Grenz Glacier. With a col depth of over 100 metres it also secures the right to be described as an independent summit. The ascent is made comparatively harmless through the closeness of the Marghérita Hut – as far as ascents of 4000ers can be generally harmless. When Joseph Zumstein and his retinue undertook the first ascent on 1 August 1820 from the snow plateau of the Colle Gnifetti, after climbing the Grenz Glacier, this was still one of the most remote places in the Alps.

Difficulties: F. Easy going on snow with, just before the summit, a few metres at 40° with some rock.

Effort: Anyone who has made the ascent of the Signalkuppe behind him, will knock off 111mH from the Colle Gnifetti at any convenient moment.

Dangers: In bad visibility on the Colle Gnifetti, very careful route-finding essential.

Pleasures: Another really high summit 'done'. And what a view.

Maps, travel, hut climb: See Signalkuppe.

Summit climb from the Marghérita Hut: Go down to the Colle Gnifetti in a few minutes. From there, climb north-westwards, finally on small ridge to the summit.

View: To the north close enough to touch the summit block of the Dufourspitze, to the east the 2400-metre drop into the Macugnaga valley, to the south the Signalkuppe and behind that the expanses of the plain of the River Po and to the west the mountains of the central chain, from the mini-4000ers like Parrotspitze, Ludwigshöhe and Schwarzhorn over the bulky Liskamm and the wall of the Breithorn to Matterhorn and Dent Blanche.

Adjacent peaks: The snowy hump **P.4463** at the base of the South-West Ridge is quickly and easily reached from the Colle Gnifetti.

Other worthwhile routes: *North Ridge* from the frontier saddle (snow ridge corniced on left with rock steps of II, mixed, 30 mins). *Traverse from the Dufourspitze across the frontier saddle* (AD, III and II, 2 hrs).

Signalkuppe (Punta Gnifetti), 4556m

The summit, which is indeed somewhat lower than the Zumsteinspitze, is nevertheless a prominent topographical junction between the frontier crest and the ridge crest running north over the Nordend-Strahlhorn-Mischabel group to Stalden. Seen from the plain and the foothills, the rugged rock bastion of the Signalkuppe appears as the dominating elevation. The name Punta Gnifetti recalls the pastor Giovanni Gnifetti, from the hamlet of Alagna at the foot of the mountain, and his seven guides and porters who in 1842 found today's customary ascent over the Lisjoch.

The building in 1893 of the Marghérita Hut, and inauguration by the Italian Queen Marghérita (replaced in 1980 by a gigantic, two-storied wooden box covered with sheet copper) fundamentally altered the mountaineering situation. For although this highest placed construction in Europe offers a high-level refuge in unsettled weather, it removes all the qualities of mountain solitude that this high top should rightfully possess. The intrusion is all the more unwelcome as the hut lacks an adequate sewage disposal system and it is rather incongruous to have to contend with sundry excreta on the slopes as one approaches the hut.

Difficulties: PD. A glacier plod to great height.

Effort: The 2100mH to Punta Indren are almost never climbed (buy a ticket for the railway from Alagna). From there it is 400mH to the Gnifetti Hut and a further 900mH up the glistening concave mirror of the glacier basin to the summit. A further, very unexpected effort for all under-acclimatized people is spending a night at this unusually high hut – you have been warned!

Dangers: Route-finding is problematical in bad visibility and if the track gets covered. There is a delicate crevasse zone just above the Gnifetti Hut. On the traverse below the Parrotspitze and Signalkuppe there is a slight danger from sérac-fall.

Pleasures: One moans freely about the crowd in the hut but, for all that, this is a place in which one can take in the magic of a breathtaking evening at very high altitude and morning moods at leisure, without all the rigmarole and paraphernalia of bivouacing.

Maps: The first part of the described route does not appear on the Swiss Maps. LKS 1348 Zermatt (Signalkuppe-Parrotspitze-Liskamm ends at the Italian-Swiss border), LKS 1:50,000 sheets 284 Mischabel and 294 Gressoney, also LKS 5006 Matterhorn-Mischabel (further south to just take in Piramide Vincent). For sketches, see Dufourspitze and Ludwigshöhe.

Travel: From the south, by rail to Varallo (456m) via Borgosesia. To here by car from the Simplon Pass via Domodossola and Omegna/Lago d'Orta-Passo La Colma (942m), then up the Sesia valley (also by bus) 35km to *Alagna* (1190m, tourist resort, camping).

Hut climb: *From Alagna*, nowadays scarcely anyone resists the temptation of the cableway. Ascent on foot, first of all from the upper end of the town via the Rusa district, up through the wood beneath the cableway, then climb the whole Olenbach valley to the Colle D'Olen (2864m, 4 hrs). Turn the north-lying Corno del Camoscio eastwards on the path and after that continue on the crest almost as far as Monte Oliveto/Stolemberg. The summit block of this is turned on the west side on a path heading downwards to the Col de la Pisse. Continue northwards on a ridge (past a ruined hut) and opposite a cairn cross a notch to the Indren Glacier. Up over this to the Punta Indren (3260m, ugly mountain station of the Alagna cableway; on foot from there 6 hrs).

Traverse north-west across the ski-ravaged glacier, then over a rock and rubble step obliquely up the path to moraine slopes. These soon lead to the *Cittá di Mantova Hut* (3498m, BV Gressoney, 112 B, managed from the end of March to mid-April, and mid-June to mid-September, Tel. 0163-78 150), 1 hr from Punta Indren.

Continue up over the moraine slopes, then traverse the reduced tongue of the Garstelet Glacier and over a rocky face to the *Gnifetti Hut* lying between the small Garstelet Glacier and contorted ice stream of the Lis Orientale Glacier

(3647m,; CAI, 277 B, managed from mid-April to mid-September, Tel. 0163-78 015).

From Zermatt, first of all go to the *Monte Rosa Hut* (see Dufourspitze). From there, as to the Dufourspitze, up the path over the Plattje, then go south-east past P.3109 and move right to the Grenz Glacier. Ascend this (many crevasses) to P.3472 at the foot of a rock island and pass this close to its south side to go up to P.3699. Continue up south-eastwards to below the Parrotspitze. Here one joins the route from the Gnifetti Hut (6-7 hrs from the Monte Rosa Hut).

Summit route from the Gnifetti Hut: Go north-east up the glacier which is disrupted by deep crevasses where the Garstelet Glacier branches off. Then head up west of Piramide Vincent, towards the Lisjoch. Before reaching this, just after passing the rock island of the Balmenhorn and the Schwarzhorn/Corno Nero, work up to the east to gain the flat saddle between the Ludwigshöhe and the flat glacier top P.4252. Now traverse the slopes under the North Face of the Ludwigshöhe and Parrotspitze into a wide glacier basin and work up obliquely left (north-west) under the Signalkuppe to gain the Colle Gnifetti. From there climbing obliquely and easily south-east to the summit of the Signalkuppe.

View: To the west are the small Monte Rosa 4000ers and after that Liskamm, Matterhorn, Dent Blanche and Zinalrothorn, to the north, close enough to touch, are the Dufourspitze, Zumsteinspitze and Nordend (with the upper part of the East Face), as well as in the distance Mischabel group and Strahlhorn. From the narrow terrace of the south side there is a dizzily exciting view down the rocky South Face and over the foothills to the expanses of the plain of the River Po. The breathtaking view eastwards down the Signalgrat is best viewed from the lavatory window of the hut.

Adjacent peaks: On the East Ridge there is, close under the hut, a prominent gendarme and near the Passo Signal the ridge summit P.3769. The elevations situated to the south-west are all rather unsatisfactorily counted as independent summits.

Other worthwhile routes: *South-West Ridge* (I and snow to 45°, 250mH from the Seserjoch, 1 hr).

East Ridge or Cresta Signal (III and II, mixed, almost 1000mH, 6 hrs from Resegotti Bivouac, with very long approach of 2000mH, 7 hrs from Alagna).

Parrotspitze, 4436m

The thoroughly independent summit south-west of the Signal-kuppe, with a col depth of 140 metres, is mostly only climbed in connection with this, usually as a traverse. From the west, it appears as a symmetrical snow pyramid with sharp cut summit ridge, from the south as a puzzlingly dark rock mountain. The first ascent was made in 1863 by the guides Melchior Anderegg and Peter Perren with their clients R.J.S. MacDonald, F. Crauford Grove and M. Woodmass.

Difficulties: PD. An exposed snow ridge.
Effort: From the ordinary ascent to the Signalkuppe additionally 170mH, 1 hr for ascent and descent.
Dangers: Observe the usual cautions, particularly on the summit ridge.
Pleasures: Elegant summit ridge.

Maps, sketches, travel, approaches: See Signalkuppe.
Summit climb: From the ascent track to the Signalkuppe, and before reaching this, move up to the Seserjoch (4296m, between Signalkuppe and Parrotspitze) and then follow the initially broad North-East Ridge to the summit.
View: Restricted by the nearby and higher Signalkuppe and Zumsteinspitze.
Other worthwhile routes: *West Ridge* (a snow knife-edge, to 40°, 1 hr which can also be conveniently added to the ascent from the Gnifetti Hut).
North-North-West Face (50° snow/ice, 200mH, small but nice).

Looking south from the summit of Monte Rosa (Dufourspitze) over the Zumsteinspitze to the Signalkuppe (left) and the Parrotspitze (right).

Ludwigshöhe, 4341m

A less independent, snowed-over hump to the south-west of the
Parrotspitze and separated from this by the Piodejoch. Mostly
visited only in combination with the neighbouring summits on the
descent (or ascent) from the Signalkuppe. First climbed by the
surveyor Ludwig van Welden and several companions in 1822.

Difficulties: F. Snow to 40°.
Effort: Slight, 48mH and 20 mins extra.
Dangers: Scarcely any.
Pleasures: Another 4000er crossed off.

Approach: See Signalkuppe, then at pleasure and easy.
Adjacent peaks: The glacier hump **P.4252** to the north-west
requires only eight metres of climbing in the opposite direction.

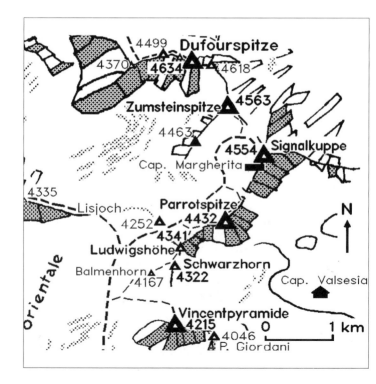

Schwarzhorn (Corno Nero), 4322m

Indeed, also not a very independent summit but in its form a prominent rock top in a beautiful position south of the Ludwigshöhe. First ascent in 1873 by Marco Maglioni and Albert de Rothschild with considerable expense of guides and porters.

Difficulties: PD. Short but hearty, snow to 50° and some rock.

Effort: Additional height difference from the route to the Signalkuppe about 30mH, 30 mins extra (from the Gnifetti Hut 720mH, 2-3 hrs).

Dangers: Scarcely any. The steep slope has run-out.

Pleasures: Attractive belvedere. Maps and approach: See Signalkuppe.

Ascent: Over the steep but short North-West Face or the rocky South-West Ridge (I) to the summit.

Balmenhorn, 4167m

A 4000er it may be, mountain it is not, but this little rock island is persistently and unnaturally included in lists of routes. In any case there are a couple of dozen more prominent adjacent peaks exactly like this nunatak – if a need for the manufacture of more 4000ers really does exist. Moreover, the fact that this pinnacle, rising scarcely a dozen metres, is decorated with a gigantic statue of Christ and a, usually horribly filthy, bivouac box does not raise its Alpine significance one iota.

Approach: See Signalkuppe, before reaching the Lisjoch, keep more distinctly to the east. From Gnifetti Hut 560mH (1-2 hrs).

Vincent Piramide, 4215m

This summit lying south of the main crest beyond the Schwarzhorn is indeed lower but far more independent than the elevations on this part of the main crest. Due to the proximity of the Gnifetti Hut, it offers an ideal acclimatization excursion or a short climb in unsettled weather. The first ascent was made in 1819 by the then owner of the gold mines around Alagna, Johann Nikolaus Vincent, with two of his mountain folk and a hunter.

Difficulties: PD. Simple snow slopes.
Effort: From the Gnifetti Hut, 600mH ascent (2 hrs).
Dangers: On the glacier the customary caution is advisable, especially in the crevasse system immediately behind the hut.
Pleasures: A beautiful prelude to bigger things, be it in days to follow or on the same day, with the traverse also of the summits to the Signalkuppe, which look appetizing from this outlier. Alternatively it is a summit to complete the traverse when already somewhat tired but giving a good opportunity for a retrospective view of the day's achievements.

The view south-east from the Liskamm to Vincent Piramide and Balmenhorn.

Looking east from the Breithorn to the Monte Rosa group. From left to right: Nordend, Dufourspitze (in between the Monte Rosa Glacier over which the ordinary route leads), Zumsteinspitze with the Grenz Glacier in front, Signalkuppe, Liskamm West Peak, Liskamm East Peak and Schneedomspitze. In front of that is the Felikjoch and in the foreground the Breithorn Central Peak with the Roccia Nera beyond.

Maps, travel, hut climb: See Signalkuppe.

Summit climb: As for the Signalkuppe to below the Balmenhorn. Turn right and work east to the Colle Vincent and from there take the north slope to the summit.

View: The peak offers a good view of the main crest and the southern foothills.

Adjacent peaks: P.4046 on the South-East Ridge haunts lists of 4000ers under the designation Punta Giordani but only imposters will celebrate this shoulder as a 'summit'.

Other worthwhile routes: *South-West Face* (PD+, pitches of I, snow to 35°, 2 hrs from Gnifetti Hut).

The 20km section of the frontier crest above Zermatt carries a parade of mountains with very differing claims and very different development. But each of them is rewarding in its way.

Liskamm, 4527m

This mighty five-kilometre ridge is notorious on account of its cornices, but its dimensions alone make it a goal to be taken very seriously. The East Summit rises 50 metres higher then the West Summit, about a kilometre away. The faces look very different: the South is predominately rocky and rugged and quite small, rising just a few hundred metres above the névé basin of the Ghiacciaio del Lis, the North, by contrast, is 700 to 1100 metres high, a steep, hostile wall of rock and ice above the crevasse and sérac labyrinths of the Grenz Glacier.

The first ascent of the main peak was made in 1861 by an army of six Swiss guides and eight British tourists (led by Franz Lochmatter), who followed a route up over the South-East Ridge. Three years later the guides Jakob Anderegg and Franz Biner with Leslie Stephen and Edward Buxton mastered the first traverse of the entire summit ridge (from west to east). It was on this ridge that, in 1877, the first party fell to their deaths when a cornice broke, thereby founding the dark reputation which the mountain has enjoyed ever since. The ideal line, and objectively a very safe climb, is by the North Rib of the East Summit. This was climbed first in 1890 by the celebrated Engadine guide Christian Klucker with his regular employer Ludwig Norman-Neruda and Josef Reinstadler.

Difficulties: AD. Snow or ice to 45°, very exposed. Here less technical ability is required than endurance, constant surefootedness and good mountain judgement.
Effort: Hut climb from Punta Indren 350mH (from the valley 2420m), summit climb 920mH (4-5 hrs), of that 350mH (2-3 hrs) on the snow ridge.

Liskamm from the north-east (from the ascent to the Signalkuppe).

Dangers: The mountain is rightly ill-famed on account of its often (especially between the East and West peaks) double-sided cornices. For that reason it is essential to move on a long rope and to stay carefully below the cornice fracture line. Above all take care not simply to paddle along previous tracks without assessing carefully whether they follow a sensible line. When in doubt, one more ice screw cannot hurt. In bad visibility, particular caution should be observed!

Pleasures: The splendid feeling of being underway on one of the most beautiful ice peaks in the Alps with tremendous scenery all around.

Maps, travel, hut climb: To the Gnifetti Hut – see Signalkuppe.

Summit climb by the East Ridge: First of all proceed as for Signalkuppe, but go directly to the Lisjoch (4151m). Climb south of a rock hump (P.4177) and up over the snow knife-edge to the East Shoulder Summit (P.4335). Continue along the almost horizontal ridge traverse keeping well down on the north side (tremendous cornices to the south) to the summit block. There, still on the north side, make another steep climb (often on bare ice) up to the connecting point of the East Ridge with the rocky South Ridge. Go right along the narrow ridge over rock and snow to reach the East Summit (P.4527).

View: To the north-east and east the Monte Rosa peaks and peaklets are set out high above the ice wastes of the Gorner, Monte Rosa and Grenz Glaciers. To the south are the Italian foothills and plain. To the west, beyond the West Summit, Castor and Pollux can be seen as well as the Breithorn. To the north-west the Weisshorn is the most dominant peak.

Adjacent peaks: The truly independent **West Summit P.4479** is most easily climbed from the Felikjoch via its South-West Ridge and this also allows the **South-West Ridge Summit P.4201** and the **Western Fore-Summit P.4417** to be taken in on the same trip. The not very independent **East Shoulder Summit P.4335** (Cima di Scoperta) has already been mentioned. There is a further insignificant ridge hump east of the West Summit on the connecting ridge (**about 4450m**). Finally, there is the rounded hump of the **Naso** (**4273m**) situated below the pronounced upper section of the South Ridge.

Other worthwhile routes: *Traverse* (PD+ with pitches of II, a long, narrow, snow and rock ridge, cornices on both sides, 2 hrs from summit to summit, 4-5 hrs from Lisjoch to Felikjoch or the other way round.

Approach from the Monte Rosa Hut over the Grenz Glacier to the Lisjoch (long glacier route, 5-6 hrs, crevasses, usually without track and best left alone in bad visibility when one can quickly despair!).

The North Face of the East Summit – the Norman-Neruda Route or Klucker Rib (D, III, ice to 50°, 3-6 hrs from the foot of the face).

Guidebook: Pennine Alps Central (The Alpine Club, 1975).

Castor, 4228m

The south-easterly and higher of the Zwillinge (Twins) rises west of the Felikjoch as a symmetrical, predominantly white pyramid. In contrast with the mighty mountain masses of Liskamm and Breithorn the pair, named after the heroes of Greek mythology or a constellation, look modest. The challenge lies less in the summit ascent itself, but rather in solving the problems of the approaches (which, particularly from the north, are anything but harmless) and to arrive at the peaks early enough to make a dual ascent in safety.

The first ascent was made in 1861 by the Chamonix guide Michel Croz with William Mathews and F.W. Jacomb using the South-East Ridge.

Difficulties: PD. Snow or ice to 35°.

Effort: Hut climb to the Quintino Sella Hut from Gressoney la Trinité 1970mH (6 hrs, or using the chair lift to the Colle Bettaforca 920mH – 3 hrs), summit climb 650mH (2-3 hrs). Alternative way from the cableway terminus Klein Matterhorn 700mH (4 hrs).

Dangers: The typical glacier and snow slope problems. The south-west slopes are occasionally avalanche prone.

Pleasures: For people who want to restrict themselves to the less exacting of the high goals, here is one!

Maps: For the approach from the Klein Matterhorn LKS 1348 Zermatt, also LKS 5006 Matterhorn-Mischabel, cf. Breithorn sketch; for approach from south 1:50,000 LKS 294 Gressoney. For sketch, see Pollux.

Travel: From the south by rail to Pont St Martin in the Aosta valley, from there 35km post bus or passenger car to *Gressoney la Trinité* (1624m, tourist resort, still in part a German speaking enclave of the Valais) or by rail to Verrès in the Aosta valley and then 31km on a little road up to *San Giacomo* (1689m, small place at the end of the Valle d'Ayas). From the north by rail to *Zermatt* (1606m, see Dufourspitze) and cableway to the Klein Matterhorn.

Hut climbs: *From Gressoney la Trinité to the Quintino Sella Hut:* First of all, follow the footpath on the eastern bank of the Lis, after ten minutes cross the stream and on the other side up to the Kapelle St Anna. Continue over alpine pastures to

Alm Sitten and up to the Bettliner Pass/Fourcla Bettaforca (2672m, on foot 3 hrs; to here from S. Giacomo in 3 hrs; also chair lift from Stával, 3km up the valley from Gressoney). Now go northwards on a path, partly over debris and rock ridges (climbing aids) for a further 3 hrs up to the *Quintino Sella Hut* which lies on the south of Punta Perazzi on the rock ridge between Piccola Ghiacciaio di Verra (west) and Ghiacciaio di Felik (east) (3587m, CAI Bella, 140 B, managed from the end of June to mid-September, Tel. 0125-36 61 13).

Summit climb by the South-East Ridge: From the Sella Hut on the Felik Glacier, head north-east round Punta Perazzi and, keeping right, ascend to the Felikjoch on the broad ridge descending from P.4093. Leave the lowest point of the col on the right. Go up left on the South-East Ridge of Castor, practically without technical difficulties but with care on account of potential cornices, crossing the South-East Summit (Felikhorn or Punta Felik, 4174m) and a fore-summit to gain the highest point.

From the Klein Matterhorn station: To the Zwillingsjoch (2-3 hrs, see Pollux). From there, climb south-east obliquely up the South-West Face to the upper part of the South-West Ridge and follow that to the summit (400mH, 2 hrs, see map opposite and photo on page 142; when there is danger of avalanches on the south side, take the North-West Ridge, AD).

View: This is dominated by the nearby Liskamm and the glacier scenery below to both north and south.

Adjacent peaks: Apart from the already mentioned South-East Ridge tops – the **South-East fore-summit (c. 4185m)** and the **Felikhorn (4174m)** as well as the **Felikjoch-Kuppe (P.4093)** – there is also a **North Summit P.4205**. It is reached from the summit over the snow ridge quickly and without difficulty.

Other worthwhile routes: *South-West Ridge* (D, climbing on firm rock to IV, approach from the Sella Hut over the saddle north of Punta Perazzi, occasionally complicated as far as the start of the climb, 2 hrs, another approach is from the Mezzalama Hut, 720mH, 5 hrs).

The northern approach to the Felikjoch or Zwillingsjoch from the Monte Rosa Hut after an adventurous traverse of the Zwillings Glacier.

Guidebook: Pennine Alps Central (The Alpine Club, 1975).

Pollux, 4092m

The smaller neighbour of Castor, most pleasantly approached by the Klein Matterhorn cableway or the Mezzalama Hut. First climbed in 1864 by Peter Taugwalder senior with Jules Jacot.

Difficulties: PD. Pitches of II, mostly I and snow to 45°.

Effort: From the Klein Matterhorn station 600mH, 3-4 hrs to the summit. On the way back allow the same time or longer on a softening glacier.

Dangers: The customary use of the cableway to the very high starting point can induce unacclimatized people to over-tax themselves. Once started it is essential to move rapidly to allow a return to be made in reasonable snow conditions. On the glacier the customary caution is advisable, particularly on the return. In bad visibility and if the track is lost this becomes an exciting expedition.

Pleasures: Anyone who can put aside the fact that by this route only a fraction of the whole mountain is climbed, enjoys the additional summit in his collection. Anyone who wants to climb it thoroughly can choose the North Ridge or traverse the summit in the course of a traverse from Monte Rosa over the Liskamm and the Breithorn – if weather, conditions and personal fitness allow.

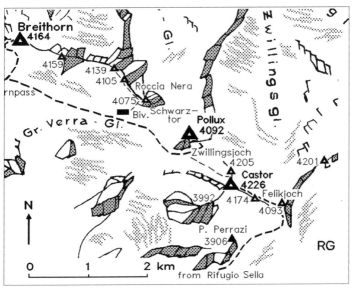

Maps: LKS 1348 Zermatt, LKS 5006 Matterhorn-Mischabel. See also Breithorn sketch.

Travel: To *Zermatt*, see Dufourspitze. From Zermatt, cableway to the Klein Matterhorn, Tel. 028-67 13 16 or 67 12 52. Also from the south from San Giacomo/St Jacques (see Castor) in 5 hrs to the Mezzalama Hut (3036m, CAI, 34 B) and from there over the glacier in 3 hrs to the Zwillingsjoch.

Summit climb by the South-East Ridge: From the terminus (3820m, no overnight stay possible), first of all go down to the saddle (3796m) in front of the Breithorn plateau and then head east on the broad track towards the Breithorn. Instead of climbing up, continue eastwards over the Breithornpass (3824m) and along under the south side of the Breithorn, below the crevasse zones of the upper Ghiacciaio di Verra. Pass below the rock island with the Cesare e Giorgio Rossi Bivouac (3750m) and the slope to the easily reachable Schwarztor. Continue under the rocky south-west spur of Pollux and move round and up to the Zwillingsjoch (Passo di Verra, 3845m; 2-3 hrs from the cableway). Now climb the, often icy, steep slope on the left (west) to the loose rocks of the South-East Ridge, which leads very airily to the summit (1 hr from the col).

View: Especially impressive, are the nearby Liskamm and Castor as well as the eastern summits of the Breithorn crest; and the glaciers below.

Other worthwhile routes: *North-West Ridge* (PD, ice 45°, rock with wire rope pitch, 360mH (1-2 hrs) from the Schwarztor). *North Ridge* (AD, large-scale classic climb over snow or ice to 50°, 1350mH, 5 hrs from the Monte Rosa Hut).

Guidebook: Pennine Alps Central (The Alpine Club, 1975).

Liskamm, Pollux and Castor from the summit of the Breithorn.

Breithorn, 4164m

From the north this appears as a magnificient two-and-a-half kilometre mountain wall. Since the first ascent in 1813 by Henry Maynard, Joseph-Marie Couttet, Jean Gras, Jean-Baptiste and Jean-Jacques Erin, the approach has changed in several respects. The area between Matterhorn and Breithorn with the Theodulepass and Testa Grigia is filled from both north and south to such a degree with lifts and cableways, that scarcely anyone still has any desire to climb up there on foot. Those who wish to climb the Breithorn usually take one of these cableways. For those who relish the beauty and remoteness of an unspoiled mountain the ascent (of the last few hundred metres) of the most climbed 4000er, by the ordinary route will be more masochism than pleasure.

Monte Rosa, Liskamm and Breithorn from the path to the Rothorn Hut.

Difficulties: PD–. This is the typical slouch 4000er. However, the snow slope is always at about 35° and sometimes icy, so crampons are essential.

Effort: 350mH climb from the mountain station (1-2 hrs).

Dangers: Glaciers always have crevasses. In bad visibility and loss of tracks, one can go astray very successfully on these wide, featureless slopes and if these risks are under-estimated, even on such a popular mountain, one can easily get lost.

Pleasures: After the experience of such a (usually) crowded climb as the Breithorn ordinary route, any other ascent is especially enjoyable.

Maps: LKS 1348 Zermatt, also LKS 5006 Matterhorn-Mischabel.

Travel: To Zermatt, see Dufourspitze. From Zermatt, cableway to the Klein Matterhorn (3820m, the mountain station does not affect the sky-line as it is below the summit and in part is set into the mountain), Tel. 028-67 13 16 or 67 12 52. From the south, also by rail through the Aosta valley to Châtillon and from there by bus or car 26km to Breuil (Cervinia, 2006m, an elegant tourist resort). From there, cableway to the Testa Grigia (3480m, from there 1-2 hrs to the Breithornpass).

Hut climb: From Zermatt, first of all go by the same route as for the Hörnli Hut (see Matterhorn) to the houses of Hermettji, then head south (past the remains of the Furgg cableway station) traversing the slopes to reach and climb the valley of the Furggbach. The path goes up the spur on the left of the river. Steeply up past the Trackener Steg cableway station to reach the *Gandegg Hut* after a four hour slog from Zermatt. (3029m, private, 30 B, managed in summer, Tel. 028-67 21 96).

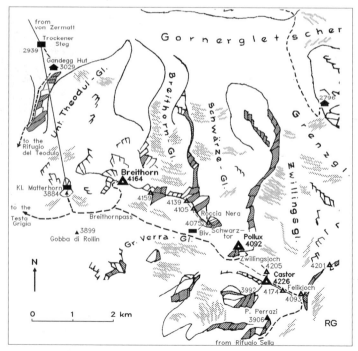

Obergabelhorn seen from the Montets Hut to the north.

‹‹ On the Zinalrothorn.   Dent d'Hérens from the Dent Blanche South Ridge. ›

Approaching the Grand Gendarme on the South Ridge of the Dent Blanche.

Monte Rosa – on the Satteltole, with Sattel (P.4359) ahead and Dufourspitze on the left.

The view back to the Monte Rosa Glacier from the Plattje.

Looking along the summit ridge of the Dufourspitze to the western fore-summit.

Above: The Monte Rosa peaks from the Signalkuppe – Zumsteinspitze (left) Dufourspitze and Nordend (right) with the upper part of the East Face on the right. The Mischabel group is in the distance.

Below: The view west from the Signalkuppe to Liskamm, with the Lisjoch and the upper Grenz Glacier below.

Descending the Moseley Slab on the Hornli Ridge.

On the shoulder of the Hornli Ridge with the Obergabelhorn in the distance. ››

The view down the icy summit slopes of the Matterhorn.

Mont Blanc at first light, seen from the Col du Meitin.

The same view (as above) at mid-day, after a Grand Combin ascent.

Descending the North-West Face of the Grand Combin.

The steep section through the sérac band on the North-West Face of the Grand Combin.

Approaching the summit of Mont Maudit.

Aiguille du Midi and Aiguille Verte (right), from the North-East Face of Mont Blanc du Tacul.

Mont Blanc from Chamonix, in the last of the evening light.

The summit dome of Mont Blanc from Mont Maudit.

On the summit of Mont Maudit, the Bosses Ridge behind.

Glacier des Bossons. ››

Dôme du Goûter from Mont Maudit.

Continue along the rocky eastern edge of the Oberer Theodul Glacier, then traverse this south-westwards across the glacier under the Theodulhorn to reach the Theodulpass and the *Theodul Hut* (6 hrs from Zermatt – 3327m, CAI, 86 B, managed from April to September, Tel. 0166-94 94 00). From here follow the ski lifts to the Testa Grigia, the follow the lift south-eastwards and finally climb north-east over the glacier (crevasses) to the Breithorn plateau to join the route from Klein Matterhorn (2 hrs from the hut).

Summit climb: From the station on the Klein Matterhorn (3820m, no overnight possibility) go through the tunnel and follow the lift down towards the saddle (3796m) in front of the Breithorn Plateau. From there head east on the broad track to the Breithornpass to tackle the climb up the steepening south-west slope, steadily working across left to the broad South-West Ridge (steep drops on the left!). This leads to the summit of the Breithorn.

View: On a beautiful day the swarm of people perhaps can be temporarily forgotten. To the west the splendid rock pyramid of the Matterhorn dominates, to the east Liskamm and Monte Rosa with their extensive ice streams, plus, to the north-west Dent Blanche, Obergabelhorn, Zinalrothorn and Weisshorn group and, to the north-east, the Mischabel group and Rimpfischhorn.

Adjacent peaks: The **Central Summit (4159m)** is reached on the ridge (cornices) without difficulties in about 1 hr. Further east the **Breithorn Twins (4139m, 4106m)** as well as the **Schwarzfluh/Roccia Nera (4075m)** are better climbed from the Cesare e Giorgio Rossi Bivouac (see Pollux).

Other worthwhile routes: *Traverse of the Breithorn crest* (AD, in part III, mixed, corniced ridges, usually done from east to west, 8-9 hrs from the Cesare e Giorgio Rossi Bivouac to the West Summit).
North Ridge or Triftjigrat (AD, rock III and II, mixed, longer passages of ice to 55°, large-scale classic ridge, 1150mH, 8 hrs from the Gandegg Hut).
North Ridge of the Breithorn Twins or Younggrat (D, to IV, distinctly more demanding than Triftjigrat, 1250mH, 9-10 hrs from the Gandegg Hut).
Guidebook: Pennine Alps Central (The Alpine Club, 1975).

Matterhorn, 4478m

This celebrated rock pyramid is the epitome of the majestic peak and is among the most famous mountains in the world, portrayed in calenders, books, films and postcards and correspondingly overcrowded. But these factors do not deter most climbers, who wish to climb the mountain sooner or later. This includes those who think they can resist its brash notoriety, a resolve easy to maintain until they actually see the mountain.

The dramatic history of its ascent has contributed to its fame. The race, into which the first ascent attempts degenerated, was decided by the obsessed Edward Whymper and his companions, Lord Francis Douglas, Charles Hudson, Douglas Hadow, as well as the guides Michel Croz (from Chamonix) and Peter (father and son) Taugwalder (from Zermatt) on 14 July 1865 after ascending the North-East (Hörnli) Ridge. Nevertheless, after an accident on the descent, only Whymper and the two Taugwalders returned (the broken rope is still to be seen in Zermatt's Alpine museum). The considerably more difficult Italian Ridge (Liongrat) was mastered three days later by Whymper's former allies and rivals Jean-Antoine Carrel and his Italian friends. The first ascent of the splendid (and still unspoilt by climbing aids) Zmutt Ridge fell to the legendary guide Alexander Burgener, with his colleagues Johann Petrus and A. Gentinetta and the brilliant Albert Frederick Mummery. The North Face, climbed by the brothers Franz and Toni Schmid in the summer of 1931, also made headlines, as well as its first winter ascent and the first survived ski descent.

Difficulties: AD−. One of the hardest 4000er ordinary routes, less for the difficulty of individual pitches than the length of the route and the care demanded. Even with the use of the fixed ropes on the summit block, there are passages III−, mostly II (very sustained) and I (if one declines to use the fixed ropes there are pitches of IV and IV+, at great height and hence correspondingly strenuous). On the shoulder and summit slope there are difficulties on mixed ground.

The rock on the ridge provides good coarse holds and is thoroughly enjoyable to climb in dry conditions, but on the faces

Matterhorn from the east with the Hörnli Ridge on the right and the Italian Ridge on the left.

it is slabby and often interspersed with marl. Route-finding is easy following the polished rock, but in wet or snow this smoothness creates additional difficulties which quickly make the Hörnli route too difficult for climbers of average ability, because of its sheer length. There are several variations on the lower part of the route.

Effort: The climb to the Schwarzsee is 950mH (2-3 hrs) or take the cableway. From the Schwarzsee to the Hörnli Hut is 700mH (2 hrs), the summit climb is 1200mH (c.1700m of climbing, 5-6 hrs).

Dangers: There have been approximately 500 deaths on the Matterhorn and this fact sends a clear message. The main danger is the hectic state into which many people only too easily drive themselves and the muddle brought about in moving and belaying. As most climbers move together, roped, but generally unbelayed (good natural belays being scarce), there are numerous opportunities to come to grief as a result of one's own, or other people's mistakes.

That is especially true of the numerous unavoidable overtaking and meeting manouevres.

A second substantial danger is the considerable length of the climb which, especially with the onset of bad weather, makes route-finding harder and ensnares many, most particularly those who are climbing at their limit. Although most of the original loose rock has now been cleared there are still plenty of opportunities for dislodging rocks, so stone-fall, even though localised, is another serious problem.

A further unusual difficulty is the 'polished' fixed ropes which are only anchored to the rock at long intervals and are bad to grip with gloves on account of their thickness. Regarding equipment, it is not wise to economise on warm clothing, windproofs or crampons. The Solvay Hut, built at a height of 4003m close to a notch on the ridge on the east side of the rocks, is exclusively assigned as emergency quarters in bad weather or accidents.

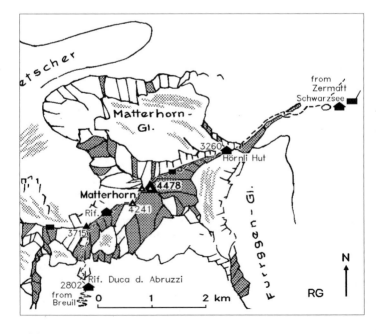

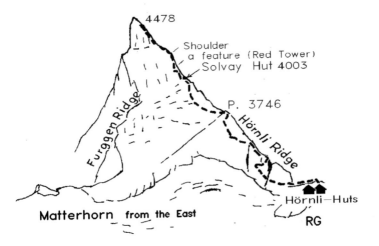

4478
Shoulder
a feature (Red Tower)
Solvay Hut 4003
P. 3746
Furggen Ridge
Hörnli Ridge
Hörnli – Huts
RG
Matterhorn from the East

Pleasures: Even though the detailed climbing is not of high quality, the ambience of this great symbolic peak and its position is still fascinating. Providing the weather is settled it is best to avoid the pre-dawn rush and start in daylight, when the route-finding and climbing will be easier and more pleasurable. The only problem with this strategy is that of passing (in ascent) the scores of descending climbers with the corresponding stone-fall and hurly burly.

Maps: LKS 1348 Zermatt and LKS 1347 Matterhorn, also LKS 5006 Matterhorn-Mischabel.
Travel: Valley locality is *Zermatt*, see Dufourspitze.
Hut climb: From Zermatt railway station walk through the town and head up the valley to Winkelmatten. From there cableways lead to the Schwarzsee. Those who resist these temptations follow the western bank of the Mattervisp to the junction of the Zmuttbach. Follow that for about 600m, then cross the bridge to the Zum See district (1766m). First of all, continue on the track in the direction of Stafelalp, but at the first fork go left up the path through the wood to Hermettji (2053m). Here, continue right (many bends) up the ridge to the Schwarzsee Hotel (2584m) and the Schwarzsee (2-3 hrs). Continue up to the west on the broad path over grassy humps and moraine debris to the dark rock wall of the Hirli. Before reaching that, first ascend left then

cut back right to gain the ridge. The 'Horn' is now very close. The path leads up, with numerous short bends, to gain the shoulder with the Hotel Belvedere and the *Hörnli Hut* (3260m, SAC Section Monte Rosa, 60 B, usually overcrowded; managed from mid-June to mid-September, Tel. 028-67 27 69).

Summit route by the Hörnli Ridge: Generally the route keeps a little to the left (12m) of the ridge on the east side. Only above the Solvay Hut does one keep more generally to the ridge edge. If one wishes to start in the dark, an evening reconnaissance of the start of the climb and its continuation is advisable.

From the Hörnli Hut, follow a horizontal ridge to a step. Move up this obliquely left (fixed rope) and traverse left (tracks) to a shoulder on the East Face. First of all ascend a little further in the direction of the ridge and then again traverse left to the East Face. There, cross a couloir and traverse further to a second couloir. Go up that for about 25m and then move on to a rock rib on the left (right of a third couloir) and follow this back to the ridge. On the ridge, climb about 100mH on good holds (tracks, crampon scratches) as far as a ledge of yellowish rock. Follow this left on the face to its end. Zig-zag directly up to the ridge to a rock tower which bars the way (remains of an old hut in front of it, 3818m, 2 hrs from the Hörnli Hut).

Make another long detour left up across the face to a slabby recess, cross a rock band and continue up left until below the Solvay Refuge. Climb up on increasingly steeper rock to reach the near vertical 'Moseley Slab' (III–, iron peg for belay) which goes directly up to the Solvay Hut (4003m, 3 hrs from the Hörnli Hut). Move left round the hut and go up a slabby gangway set between steeper rocks and soon move back up (the Upper Moseley Slab, III–) to regain the ridge, which is followed over blocks. Turn the Red Tower on the left and after that the ridge is followed further to the 'Shoulder' (mostly snow and ice with iron belay pegs).

Climb a short snow and ice ridge and the crest of the ridge above to gain the steep summit block. Keep on the edge using steep cracks and steps, on which thick, greasy fixed ropes obtrude as aids to heaving oneself up inelegantly. Thus one reaches the often icy summit slope and soon afterwards gain the highest point (at the eastern end of the Summit Ridge).

South-West or Italian Ridge: (AD, III and fixed ropes (without these), IV), a better climb than the Hörnli Ridge, but overall more tiring and for that reason is often done in descent). From Breuil (2006m) go to the Duca degli Abruzzi Hut (2802m, 2-3 hrs). Take the path to the Croce di Carrel and go up a gully heading obliquely left over a rock barrier to a rock ridge. Traverse to the eastern edge of the snow-field under constant threat of stone-fall and on it to a rock rib under the summit block of the Tete du Lion. Go right on ledge, crossing some gullies (stone-fall, delicate), to the Col du Lion (3580m). Keeping on the south side of the ridge, climb a succession of slabby rocks using fixed ropes to reach and climb the 'Seiler Slab' and above the vertical 12m 'Whymper Chimney', followed by more slabs (fixed ropes) leading to the Savoia Hut (only for emergencies) and the *Rifugio Carrel* (3829m, 40 B, radio telephone; 4-5 hrs from Aosta Hut).

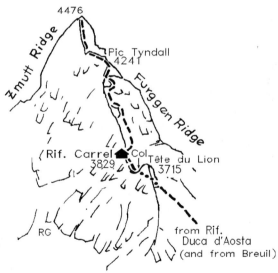

Matterhorn from the South West

Turn the pinnacle ridge above on the south side (many fixed ropes) passing the 'Mauvais Pas' (a toe ledge) and 'Linceul' (a small patch of ice) to a wall with another fixed rope. Climb this ('Corde Tyndall') to the ridge. Continue up that, turning most obstacles on the left, to the Pic Tyndall (4241m, 3 hrs). Move across the almost horizontal ridge, and cross a deep notch

('Enjambée'), to gain the summit block. Follow the obvious line of the ropes and up a rope ladder ('Echelle Jordan') to the West (Italian) Summit. A short climb along the summit ridge (with notch) leads to the main summit (5 hrs from the Carrel Hut).

View: Overwhelming – from Mont Blanc, Dent d'Hérens and Grand Combin in the west to the northern giants of Dent Blanche, Obergabelhorn, Zinalrothorn and Weisshorn to the Mischabel group with Dom, Täschhorn, Alphubel, Allalinhorn, Rimpfischhorn and Strahlhorn and further to the white mass of Monte Rosa, to the Liskamm and the Breithorn in the east. Only to the south is the distant view not sensational, but to compensate, the view down the mountain itself leaves nothing to be desired.

Adjacent peaks: The not very prominent **West Summit** (with an iron cross) is at **4476m** only slightly lower than the Swiss East Summit. The **Pic Tyndall (4241m)** on the shoulder of the South-West Ridge is traversed on the ascent of the Italian Ridge.

Other worthwhile routes: *North-West or Zmutt Ridge* (D, IV– and III, mixed, seldom in good condition, snow or ice to 50°, the great classic Matterhorn ridge without any climbing aids, 1200mH, 7-9 hrs from the Hörnli Hut).

South East or Furggen Ridge (D+/TD, IV, direct up to VI, unstable rock; 1150mH from start of climb, 8-12 hrs).

North Face (TD, steep ice and IV, or V, delicate unstable rock, one of the great classic north faces of the Alps, 1100mH, 10-12 hrs).

Guidebooks: Pennine Alps Central (The Alpine Club, 1975).

Matterhorn and Monte Rosa from the west (from the South Ridge of the Dent Blanche).

Dent d'Hérens, 4171m

Somewhat upstaged by the Matterhorn, this mountain receives comparatively little attention. It is situated in the remotest corner of the Matter valley and is similarly distant from valley bases on the Italian side. However, this a very beautifully formed mountain with elegant lines and rewarding routes, all of which make respectable sporting demands preceded by long approach marches. Today's ordinary route up the South-West Face was also the route of the first ascent in 1863 by F. Crauford Grove, W.E. Hall, R.S. MacDonald and W. Woodmass with the guides Melchior Anderegg, Peter Perren and Jean Pierre Cachat. The classic route up the two kilometre East Ridge was climbed in 1906 by Franz and Joseph Lochmatter with V.J.E. Ryan. The first ascent of the gigantic North Face, one of the first extreme ice routes, was made in 1925 by Willo Welzenbach, later to die on Nanga Parbat, and Eugen Allwein.

Difficulties: PD+. Mainly a long glacier climb, then some rock climbing to II, finally along a narrow, exposed summit ridge.
Effort: Hut climb 800mH (5-6 hrs), summit climb 1400mH (5-6 hrs).
Dangers: The customary rules of caution on glaciers must be particularly carefully observed, especially since one can scarcely count on outside help.
Pleasures: A solitary and serious mountain.

Maps: LKS 1347 Matterhorn, also LKS 5006 Matterhorn-Mischabel.
Travel: By rail or motorway to Aosta. From the main road leading to the Great St Bernhard, the road branches after about 4km to Valpelline (960m) and up to Bionaz (1606m; village, or by post bus to here, from Aosta 29km).
Hut climb: The lane is still suitable for motors for another 6km to the reservoir dam of Lac di Place Moulin. From there a one hour walk along the lakeside leads to Prarayer (2005m, hotel, only open in summer). Now follow the track (paying careful attention to the markings) up the long valley to the *Aosta Hut* (2781m, CAI Section Aosta, 24 B, managed at times from mid-June to the end of August, Tel. 0165-31 696 or 43 588). This can also be reached from Zermatt in 5-6 hrs from the Schönbiel Hut over the Col de Valpelline and Col de la Division; or, from the Val d'Arolla

from the Bertol Hut over the Col des Bouquetins.

Summit route by the South-West Face: From the hut descend a little and then head east on a path over moraines and up the northern part of the Grandes Murailles Glacier. A tiring crevasse zone is avoided on the left. After that, cross under the Tiefenmattenjoch and ascend below the flank of the West Ridge (keep well clear because of stone-fall) heading towards the foot of the South-South-West Ridge before cutting back left to about 3800m. Cross the bergschrund and climb the South-West Face over snow and easy rocks (keeping left) to gain the upper, easier part of the West Ridge. There, over blocks and steps, and finally on a narrow pinnacle ridge to the summit.

View: There is a fine view of the Matterhorn towering up to the east, with a particularly good aspects of the Italian Ridge, the West Face and the Zmutt Ridge. By contrast, the Dent Blanche towering up to the north appears distant. To the west are the mountains of Arolla and beyond that the Grand Combin.

Adjacent peaks: On the East Ridge rises the fore-summit of the **Epaule (4039m).**

Other worthwhile routes: *West Ridge* (AD–, III+ and III, mixed, from Aosta Hut 1400mH, from the Tiefenmattenjoch 600mH, 3 hrs).

North-West Face (AD, to 45°, occasionally extreme crevasses; 1500mH from Schönbiel Hut, with 850mH on the face itself).

East Ridge (D, IV and III, 700 mH, sections unstable with very long stretches of climbing, 8-10 hrs. from the Col Tournanche).

North Face (TD+, ice to 90°, rock to IV, menaced by falling ice, 1300mH, 10-15 hrs).

Guidebook: Pennine Alps Central (The Alpine Club, 1975).

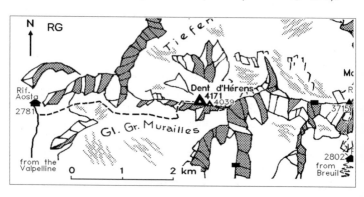

Far to the west, set apart from the other Pennine 4000ers, the Grand Combin is really a separate mountain massif which also lies on the frontier crest and forms the link between the high Pennine peaks and the Mont Blanc group.

Grand Combin, 4314m

The Grand Combin is an alpine mountain in the most beautiful sense of the word. One reaches the huts from far below, by approaches up delightful solitary valleys, and even from the huts there is still a considerable distance to go to the summit. Also the easiest of its ascents have their problems, especially that chosen for the first ascent in 1857 by Benjamin and Maurice Felley and Jouvence Bruchez and the technically easiest ascent over the 'Corridor', threatened as it is by a wall of séracs which regularly disgorge ice avalanches. An ascent by this way is like Russian Roulette. For that reason other routes are recommended here which, though technically harder, have less objective danger. The West Ridge was climbed for the first time in 1884 by C. Boisviel with D. Balleys and S. Henry, the North-West Face in 1933 by E.R. Blanchet with K. Mooser. These routes have become more popular since spring 1988, when an avalanche destroyed the Panossière Hut (since rebuilt). Ascertain in the valley the actual position regarding overnight possibilities! On the high-level traverse route from Chamonix to Zermatt the traverse of the slopes under the Col du Meitin provides the greatest technical problem which is the same as that to be overcome on this famous ski traverse.

Difficulties: Snow to 45° on the approach to the Col du Meitin from the south (serious), on the North-West Face (AD+) there is snow and ice to 50° (occasionally steeper on the séracs); on the West Ridge, (PD+) rock-climbing with passages of III and II, but mostly I, brittle, mostly mixed; on the South Face (PD+) there is unstable rock at II and mixed and snow climbing to 45°.

Effort: Hut climb from Bourg St Pierre to the Valsorey Hut 1400mH (5 hrs), the summit climb by the North-West Face is 1450mH (5 hrs) and on the return 200mH to recross the col;

by the West Ridge or South Face 1300mH (5-6 hrs).

Dangers: On the North-West Face there is danger of falling ice, but this is far less than on the 'Corridor'. On the South Face and on the approach to the Col du Meitin stone-fall is possible in fine weather and late in the day. On all the routes there are long passages of ascent and descent on steep ground to overcome, so considerable endurance and constant surefootedness are necessary. One compensation is that the West Ridge offers an (almost) glacier-free ascent. On the glaciers, observe customary precautions against crevasse falls, on the ridges in the vicinity of the summit, beware of the gigantic cornices on the south side.

Pleasures: Being underway on a really untouched range.

Maps: LKS 5003 Mont Blanc-Grand Combin.

Travel: By rail to Aosta or Orsières (via Martigny). From Aosta by bus over the Great St Bernard Pass (where the legendary St Bernard dogs and the still much bigger plush Bernhardiners are) to *Bourg St Pierre* (1632m; small place on the main road, businesses; the village can also be reached more conveniently from Orsierres or Martigny (37km).

Hut climb: From above the filling station and foreign exchange kiosk in Bourge St Pierre take a narrow track, or a small road, up into the side valley of the Valsorey stream. Where the road leads back left, continue by the stream, then soon climb the

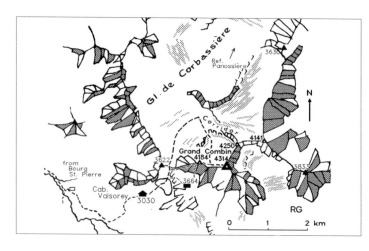

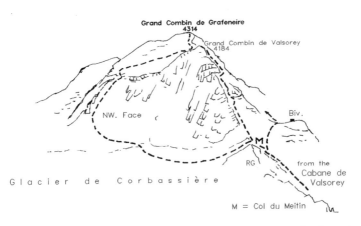

northern slope to an alm hut (1834m). Continue on the broad track on the northern slope of the valley. At the bridge (branching of the path to the Vélan Hut) stay on the north bank to soon reach the idyllic alm Chalet d'Amont (2197m). Continue in the same direction to a rocky wall, which is breached by a constructed path. After that, trend round to the east on the slope leading to the high pastures and then up a long block and debris slope to the *Valsorey Hut* which is placed on a spur (3030m, SAC Chaux de Fonds, 60 B, managed from April to September, June only at weekends, Tel. 026-49 122).

Summit climb: *To the Col du Meitin*: From the Valsorey Hut, go north-east over moraines to the small Glacier du Meitin and steeply up a snow gully (or on the easy rocks right or left of it) to the not very prominent Col du Meitin (c.3610m, 2 hrs from the hut; a little to the west is the Combin du Meitin, 3622m).

North-West Face: *From the Col du Meitin*, descend northwards into the uppermost basin of the Glacier de Corbassière keeping a respectful distance from the ice debris and avalanche remains, before crossing the bergschrund and traversing up the North-West Face to the flatter slopes of the spur above P.3406 (to here also from the Panossière Hut over the Glacier de Corbassière in 3 hrs). Move up right of the rocks (scarcely any belay possibilities) over the steep snow directly up to a break in the sérac barrier above. Through this steeply, (with or without ice, according to conditions) to the lower edge

173

of the summit plateau (P.3987). Go up this, in a slanting line to the right to gain the saddle east of the Combin de Valsorey. Then head left (east) over the slopes (gigantic cornices on the right over the South Face!) to the transmitter installed on the summit and keeping left of that, gain the highest point (**Combin de Grafeneire, 4314m**). This route is perhaps best in good snow conditions when the West Ridge may be iced up. In lean conditons, the ridge would be the best choice.

West Ridge: From the col there is initially some scrambling to the first of the three big steps. These are overcome very near the edge with the harder sections turned on the right (several possibilities). The overhang at the end of the first step is turned on the right and after that the ridge is regained by a groove. On the second step, the difficulties can also be avoided on the right using a couloir with whitish rock. After that there is a horizontal section (shoulder). The third step is climbed direct or turned on the right. Finally, scramble up the shattered ridge to reach the summit of the Combin de Valsorey (4184m). To the east of this move easily down into the wide saddle (4132m) to join the final part of the North-West Face route to the main summit.

South Face to the Combin de Valsorey: From the ascent to the Col du Meitin move up right from below the snow gully and climb steep slopes to the Plateau du Couloir (3664m, bivouac shelter) on the South Face of the Combin de Valsorey. From there climb the rather broken face (brittle rock, mixed) either keeping left to the shoulder of the West Ridge or trending across right to the saddle east of the Combin de Valsorey.

View: In the immediate vicinity, the Combin dominates all the nearby peaks. To the west is the Mont Blanc region, to the east the Zermatt 4000ers. The most interesting peaks nearby are Mont Vélan to the south-west and Mont Blanc du Cheilon to the east.

Adjacent peaks: The **Combin de Valsorey (4184m)** is traversed on the West Ridge and is easily reached when finishing the North-West Face route. On the North Ridge lie the less prominent **Aiguille du Croissant (4250m)** and, somewhat to the east, the **Combin de Tsessetta (4141m)**.

Other worthwhile routes: *North-West Face to the Combin de Valsorey* (D/D+, ice to 60°, 700mH, 5-7hrs from the foot of the face close under the Col du Meitin).

From the north-east by the Corridor (PD, technically easy but only for people who definitely want to live dangerously; from the Panossière Hut 1650mH, 6-8 hrs, of that more than 1 hr in area acutely menaced by falling ice).

The South-East Ridge (PD+, a fine route, despite some friable rock, with wonderful views; from the Amiante Hut 1335mH 6-8 hrs, from the Valsorey Hut 7-9 hrs).

Guidebook: Pennine Alps West (The Alpine Club, 1979).

On the North-West Face of the Grand Combin, the Glacier Corbassière below.

The Mont Blanc group is not the most extensive massif in the Alps, but has by far the highest peaks. It consists in the main of splendid granite, a rock that decorates the mountains with a diversity of wild, coloured sculptural forms and also provides wonderful rock climbing in the highest and most splendid situations. The main disadvantage is that with its height and situation the range is a focal point at the western (weather) end of the Alps and thus suffers from sudden and incalculably violent weather changes.

Aiguille Verte, 4122m

Elegance and difficulty determine the aura of this big peak which, with its many filigree ridges, stands in sharp contrast to the more lumpen ice masses of Mont Blanc or the rock bastions of the Jorasses. These three mountain groups stand in marvellous juxtaposition. That this slender, snow-glittering form hanging ethereally above the gothic rock splendour of its satellite the Dru, should be called 'Green Needle' is a puzzle. Perhaps it indicates that to the people of the Chamonix valley the green bases of the mountains were more nourishing and for that reason more important than the icy splendour above them in the clouds.

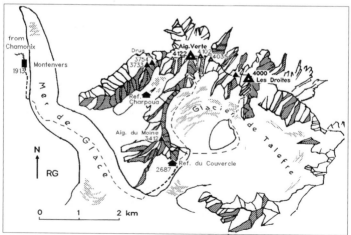

Aiguille Verte, Grande Rocheuse, Aiguille du Jardin and a part of the Droites seen from the lower Glacier de Talèfre.

The summit was reached for the first time on 29 June 1865 by the outsiders Edward Whymper and his Swiss guides Christian Almer and Franz Biener, who followed a route based on the Whymper Couloir. It released a storm of doubts in the guides' guild of Chamonix, who above all were indignant that a local guide had not also been hired. Certainly there were those in Chamonix who were capable of such ascents, as Michel Croz, M.A. Ducroz and the Zermatt guide Peter Perren proved a week later with Thomas S. Kennedy, Charles Hudson and G.C. Hodgkinson on the first ascent of the Moine Ridge.

The splendid ice climbs of the north side threw down a challenge for the ice specialists of the next generation. Already by 1876 (under more favourable ice conditions than today) the Cordier Couloir was climbed by Henri Cordier, Thomas Middlemore, John Oakley Maund with Jakob Anderegg, Johann Jaun and Andreas Maurer. The long ascent over the Montets Ridge was made in 1925 by Pierre Dalloz, Jacques Lagarde and Henri de Ségogne. The gigantic (1100m) Couturier Couloir was climbed in 1929 by Georges Charlet, A. Couttet and André Devassoux with the American Bradford Washburn by a devious line, and a more direct ascent was made three years later by Armand Charlet and Jules Simond with Marcel Couturier. Finally on this side of the mountain, the high and icy North-West or Nant Blanc Face fell to Armand Charlet and D. Plattonov in 1935.

The view from the Aiguille Verte to the Grandes Jorasses group . . .

The East-South-East Ridge over the Aiguille du Jardin and Grande Rocheuse was first traversed in 1904 by Jean Ravanel and Léon Tournier with E. Fontaine. The West Ridge fell in 1926 to A. Charlet and M. Bozon with Mlle G. de Longchamp.

Difficulties: *Whymper Couloir* (best with a generous snow cover in early summer) AD. The difficulties depend on conditions. This is a large-scale, snow and ice route with sections of 55° and an average inclination of 48°. In lean conditions the ice climbing can be very hard at the bergschrund (on descent this is often problematic with a big jump or awkward abseil manouevre). A well-established line of steps can make a considerable difference to the speed of ascent.
Moine Ridge (preferably when very dry) AD. Some mixed climbing, with rock-climbing sustained at II with passages of III.

Effort: From Montenvers by venerable rack railway. Hut climb from Montenvers 900mH (3-4 hrs), summit climb 1450mH (6-9 hrs from hut).

Dangers: On the generally very harmless Mer de Glace take great care when crossing the broad melt water gullies because they have hopelessly smooth walls and end in deep crevasses. On the Glacier de Talèfre, especially on the upper part, beware of crevasses. On the summit ridge watch carefully for cornices. The Whymper Couloir faces south and in good weather warms up correspondingly quickly, therefore a very early departure and rapid completion of the climb is essential before the

. . . and to Mont Blanc.

snow becomes rotten and the stones begin to fall. Here the saying 'speed is safety' is the guide. When the ice is very bare, the danger of stone-fall increases and then the objectively less dangerous Moine Ridge is preferable, but by either route the ascent of the mountain is a serious undertaking not to be underestimated.

Pleasures: All climbs on the Verte are big, high alpine undertakings, which guarantees excitement and class, a cache emphasised by the select few alpinists who make it to the summit.

Maps: IGN carte touristique 1:25,000, 1 Massif du Mont Blanc.

Travel: By rail or car to *Chamonix* (1030m; a bustling, cosmopolitan, tourist resort with intensive snob appeal, but also the biggest and most diverse concentration of international mountaineers in the Alps, all waiting to tackle the great climbs that tower above them. The town also offers a full range of counter attractions – bars, resturants, swimming pools and campsites for those for whom mountains alone are not enough and who must always have town life as well. The Bureau des Hautes Montagnes offers a comprehensive information service about routes and weather conditions, ENSA (Ecole Nationale de Ski et d'Alpinisme), campsites to suit all purses; above all, always full, full, full campsites, car-parks, saloons, mountain railways, huts, ordinary routes, water sports centres – all of which are expensive.

179

Hut climb: From Chamonix take the rack railway up to *Montenvers* (1876m, footpaths more or less parallel to the railway line). From the station descend southwards and finally use ladders over ice-polished slabs, to reach the Mer de Glace. Ascend first of all on the western edge, then move up to the middle of the glacier for about 3km. At the junction with the Leschaux Glacier, turn left and work across to the north bank. After traversing the debris-covered ice sections and moraines (coloured metal barrels as markers) gain iron ladders that ascend the cliffs on the left (north). Climb these over the steep, polished rocks. Then follow the path, high above the ice-fall of the Glacier de Talèfre, over grass and moraine to the *Couvercle Hut*, placed at the foot of the Aiguille Moine (2687m, the old hut is built on the historic bivouac site under the gigantic slanting roofing slab, CAF Paris, 30 + 120 B, self-service room, managed in summer, Tel. 50-53 16 94).

Summit climbs: *From the Courvercle Hut* take the path over the moraines to the western edge of the Glacier de Talèfre. Climb the glacier in a wide arc under the rock walls of the Aiguille du Moine and the connecting pinnacle ridge, to the foot of the Aiguille Verte (2 hrs). There are now two possibilities:

To reach the **Whymper Couloir** ascend to the uppermost part of the glacier. The couloir descends from the notch on the ridge between the Aiguille Verte and Grande Rocheuse. Cross the bergschrund on the right under the rocks of the Grande Rocheuse and first of all ascend a small parallel couloir. Then move left on to a rocky ridge and further above traverse to a side branch of the main couloir. Cross this too and then on the right (eastern) side of the main couloir ascend a rock rib. Where this runs out, move obliquely to the left and go directly up to the saddle in front of the Grande Rocheuse or continue obliquely left over mixed ground to the East Ridge which leads up (cornices!) to the summit.

For the **Moine Ridge**, turn left at 3350m, before reaching the Aiguille Verte, and cross the bergschrund below a conspicious, right-slanting, snow couloir at the back of a bay, right of the prominent rock pinnacle of The Cardinal. From the foot of the couloir move up ledges, heading up for about 200m to the notch between the Cardinal and Aiguille Verte (3600m).

On the ridge turn back in the direction of the Aiguille Verte. First keeping right, zig-zag up ledges and go up to the small notch of an adjacent ridge (by a five-metre gendarme at the upper end of the couloir mentioned earlier). Continue up the adjacent ridge and after that ascend obliquely right over slabs and snow patches until one can see into the Whymper Couloir. Now, climb directly back to the ridge, first up a chimney gully then zig-zagging over slabs until one reaches the ridge by a less conspicuous gendarme. Go up on the right side (east) of the ridge, turning a final tower on the east, to the summit.

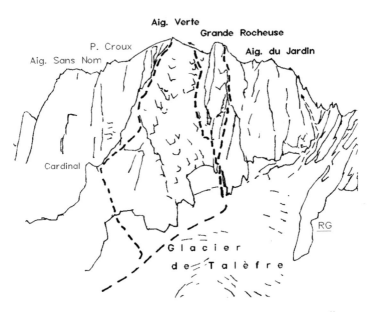

View: 'Upon the summit of the Verte . . . you see valleys, villages, fields; you see mountains interminable rolling away, lakes resting in their hollows; you hear the tinkling of the sheep-bells as it rises through the clear mountain air, and the roar of the avalanches as they descend to the valleys; but above all there is the great white dome, with its shining crest high above; with its sparkling glaciers that descend between buttresses which support them: with its brilliant snows, purer and yet purer the farther they are removed from this unclean world.' (Whymper, *Scrambles Amongst the Alps*). It only remains to add that, apart from Mont Blanc, the crest of the Jorasses to the south is equally eye-catching.

Descent: If the snow in the Whymper Couloir is already dangerous, the descent over the objectively less dangerous South Spur of the Grande Rocheuse might be considered. This looks, nevertheless, very steep and, without exact local knowledge and without a track, it is certainly difficult to locate from above. One can of course descend the Moine Ridge. If the couloir is still preferred, it is advisable to wait until the evening before descending the hardening snow (some abseil points are installed).

Adjacent peaks: On the West Ridge the **Pointe Croux (4023m)** is an insignificant gendarme which can be reached from the summit with a descent and re-ascent in about an hour. Beyond that is the Aiguille Sans Nom (3982m), a sort of buttress summit. Strictly speaking, the Grande Rocheuse and Aiguille du Jardin are also eastern fore-summits of the Aiguille Verte but these days they are usually regarded as independent 4000ers.

Other worthwhile routes: *North-West Ridge or Arête des Grands Montets* (D, rock-climbing to IV, mixed, long and high, finally with snow or ice to 50°, 900mH by c.1.7km length, 8-12 hrs from Grands Montets mountain terminus).

East-South-East or Jardin Ridge (D, a long ridge climb that crosses the Aiguille du Jardin and Grande Rocheuse with two pitches IV, 10-14 hrs from the Couvercle Hut to the summit of the Aiguille Verte.).

North-East Face or Couturier Couloir (D, large-scale ice route set at 55°, it is rare for the whole couloir to be in good condition and near the summit there can be a danger of slab avalanches even in summer, 1100mH, 4-7 hrs from bergschrund, 6-9 hrs from the Argentière Hut).

North-West or Nant Blanc Face (D+, a sustained mixed climb on rock to IV and ice to 55°, 1000mH, 12 hrs from Montenvers).

West or Sans Nom Ridge (D+, climbing to IV, mostly mixed, an especially beautiful and very long route, 10-12 hrs from the Charpoua Hut).

Guidebook: Mont Blanc Range, Vol.3 (The Alpine Club, 1976).

Grande Rocheuse, 4102m

The prominent ridge summit east of the Aiguille Verte but only separated by a col height of about 70 metres. The summit can be 'taken in' on an ascent of the Whymper Couloir with about an hour's extra effort. For a separate ascent, the less dangerous South Pillar is preferred, which in problematical conditions can also serve as a somewhat complicated descent from the Aiguille Verte. The first ascent was made in 1865 by Michel Ducroz and Michel Balmat with R. Fowler.

Difficulties: AD. Pitches of III, but mostly II.
Effort: Hut climb and summit climb, see Aiguille Verte.
Dangers: See Aiguille Verte, but the stone-fall danger is only on the lower section of the route.
Pleasures: A summit to take in on the way.

Maps, sketches, travel, hut climb: See Aiguille Verte.
Summit climb by the South Pillar: Begin as for the Whymper Couloir as far as the upper end of the rock rib left of the initial couloir. Now cross the adjacent couloir on the right and go straight up the rocks of the pillar to a gendarme (3820m). Pass this on the left (west) and 150m higher, turn a second gendarme on the right and follow the ridge of the pillar to the steep summit wall. Keeping left at first, ascend chimneys and then move more to the right and go up to reach the summit ridge about 50m east of the main summit.

Grande Rocheuse from the Aiguille Verte with the Grand Combin in the distance (left).

Aiguille du Jardin, 4035m

This is the broader ridge summit south-east of the Grande Rocheuse and separated from it by the Col Armand Charlet. The first ascent of this pinnacle, which rises only 40m above the col, was made in 1904 by Jean Ravanel and Léon Tournier with E. Fontaine during an ascent of the Jardin Ridge to the Aiguille Verte. A memorable alpine deed took place in 1932 when the peak was climbed solo by the seventy-two year old Karl Blodig, via the steep (up to 54°) North-East Couloir. Blodig was protecting his claim as the first to have climbed 'all' the 4000ers, a feat that was threatened by the nomination of these new 4000ers.

Difficulties: D. Several passages IV, mostly III and II. A large-scale, high alpine ridge-traverse with some route-finding difficulties.
Effort: From the Couvercle Hut a climb of 1400mH with a complicated line.
Dangers: A long climb over glacier followed by a rock ascent (unstable in places).
Pleasures: One of the oddest 4000ers for the obsessive peak bagger.

Maps, sketches, travel, hut climb: See Aiguille Verte.
Summit route: As for Whymper Couloir as far as under the face. Now traverse under the Grande Rocheuse and Aiguille du Jardin and then climb the right-flanking rib (east) of the snow gully that leads up to the Col de l'Aiguille Verte (3796m), or follow the gully itself if conditions are suitable. At three-quarters height, cross the snow gully to the left to a broad rock gully. Go up this keeping left (I) and continue parallel to the East Ridge. The gully then steepens to a rotten chimney (IV). This leads to a gendarme on a ridge rib further left. Climb the firm rock of this rib (III and IV), keeping left higher up, to the main ridge. This whole exercise allows one to turn the difficult lower towers of the East Ridge. Now, keeping to the edge, go first up an exposed buttress then a less steep section of ridge to a snow shoulder. From there it is a short distance to the summit.

Adjacent peaks: On the short North-West Ridge is the gendarme **Pointe Eveline (4026m)**.

Les Droites, 4000m

A broad wedge of rock and ice which reaches the magic height exactly at its East Summit. It is well-known and notorious for its fierce North Face falling to the Argentière basin, which has a row of the most extreme mixed routes in the Alps. The first ascent of the East Summit was made in 1876 to Henri Cordier, Thomas Middlemore, J. Oakley Maund with J. Jaun and A. Maurer. The almost endless climbing on the 2000-metre North-East spur was done in 1937 by Ch. Authenac and Ferdinand Tournier, and straightened in 1946 by André Contamine, Louis Lachenal, Pierre Leroux and Lionel Terray. The notoriously steep, mixed North Face, with ice to over 70°, was first conquered in 1955 by P. Corneau and M. Davaille with five bivouacs. Its original reputation for fierce difficulty has subsequently been reduced a little by rapidly improved ice gear and a string of daring solo ascents, but it still remains an exacting and serious expedition.

Difficulties: AD. Climbing to III, mixed, often with a complicated bergschrund.
Effort: From the Couvercle Hut a 700mH approach and 600mH of climbing (6-7 hrs from the hut to the summit).
Dangers: Observe all precautions, although the approach is short, the glacier and bergschrund can be awful. The rock is brittle in places.
Pleasures: Very untouched, fierce surroundings.

Maps, sketches, travel, hut climb: See Aiguille Verte.
Summit climb by the South Ridge of the East Peak: From the Couvercle Hut go north-east over the Glacier de Talèfre, to pass the moraine island 'Jardin de Talèfre' on its west side (also possible on the east side). The South Ridge of the East Peak lies east of the upper end of the 'Jardin'. The lower, ridge-like part is avoided on its west side. After overcoming the bergschrund climb a dièdre-like snow couloir on the flank, or by the rocks on its right boundary. After reaching the knife-edge of the spur, continue up an easy rock ridge to a steep wall. Climb this near the ridge over steps to reach a steep snow-field. Work up and across this (left) and finish by a snow ridge which leads to the summit ridge a little to the east of the highest point.

View: To the south-west is Mont Blanc and the pinnacled ridges of the Chamonix Aiguilles. Nearby, to the west is Aiguille Verte and its satellites. To the south the Jorasses dominate and below and to the east is the Argentière basin, famed for its top-class ice routes.

Adjacent peaks: The West Summit (3994m) is about 500m away.

Other worthwhile routes: *Traverse to the West Summit* (AD, III, mixed, 4-5 hrs).

North-East Spur (TD+, VI, V+ and V, one of the finest mixed climbs in the Alps, 1200mH, c.2000m of climbing, 12-20 hrs).

North Face (ED, Extreme ice and mixed climbing, V, A1, 63°, 1000mH, 15-22 hrs).

The North Face of the Grandes Jorasses from the Talèfre Glacier.

Grandes Jorasses, 4208m

The name is music. Heroic. This majestic ridge crest east of the bulky Mont Blanc massif though not of such great height, surpasses it in its northern and western aspects, with its wildness and elegance. The south side, though not elegant, is certainly wild, being defended by disrupted glaciers and thrusting bastions of distorted rock. The ultimate in remoteness is surely the gigantic slab triangle of the East Face dominating the wildly crevassed Frébouze Glacier. The showpiece of the whole Mont Blanc range – and indeed the Alps generally – remains the huge granite wall on the north side with its slender buttresses. The greatest of these is the Walker Spur, the highest and most unbroken buttress on the face. It ends directly at the highest point and offers by far the most ideal extreme route in the Alps, continuously difficult, without escape possibilities, but with comparatively few objective dangers in good weather. Its splendid position with an abundance of unspoiled climbing, high above the Leschaux Glacier basin completes the aura of a great classic climb set far from mountain railways and the bustle of civilization.

Even the easiest climb on the Grandes Jorasses is a demanding undertaking. It was mastered for the first time in 1865 by Edward Whymper with the famous guides Michel Croz, Christian Almer and Franz Biener. They climbed the somewhat lower Pointe Whymper because they made the ascent principally as reconnaissance for the conquest of the Aiguille Verte. The highest point was reached three years later by Horace Walker with Melchior Anderegg, Johann Jaun and Julien Grange by the ordinary route.

The North-East or Hirondelles Ridge received its first passage in 1911 when H.O. Jones and Geoffrey Winthrop Young with Joseph Knubel and Laurent Croux climbed it in descent. It was first ascended in 1927 by a big Italian party led by Adolphe Rey and Alphonse Chenoz. The South-East Ridge or Tronchey Arête, which leads from the grassy valley slopes in a long line to the summit, was first climbed in 1936 by T. Gilberti and E. Croux.

The epic attempts to conquer the North Face fill the alpine history books. It was first climbed in 1935 (after some forty attempts by various parties) by Rudolf Peters and Martin Meier who followed the Croz Spur in the middle of the face. The first ascent of the classic Walker Spur was made by the crack Italian rock climbers Riccardo Cassin, Gino Esposito and Ugo Tizzoni in 1938. Although in the years that followed several more difficult routes were added to this magnificent face not one improved on the Walker Spur in terms of climbing quality, line and scale.

Difficulties: AD−. Predominantly ice, to 45°, in part rock to II.
Effort: Hut climb 1200mH (4 hrs), summit climb 1400mH (6-7 hrs).
Dangers: In the snow basin before the summit block, there is danger of avalanches and falling ice. Otherwise take the customary precautions against crevasses and watch out for big cornices on the summit ridge.
Pleasures: A climb on one of the greatest peaks of the alps, steeped in historic associations.

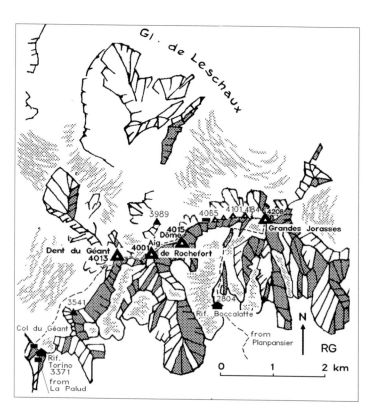

Maps: IGN, carte touristique 1:25,000, 1 Massif du Mont Blanc.

Travel: By rail from the south through the Aosta valley to Pré-St Didier. From there, 5km by bus to *Courmayeur* (1264m; the principal town on the south side of Mont Blanc, with all amenities, or on the north side through the Arve valley to Chamonix. From there by bus through the Mont Blanc tunnel to Entrèves (1306m, 2.5km from Courmayeur) and then by bus north-eastwards up the Val Ferret 3.5km to *Planpincieux* (or, *Planpansier*, 1579m, camping).

Hut climb: Take the path starting left of the church and head northwards up through sparse woods and over grassy slopes to the edge of the Torrent de Marguera gorge. Go along the gorge to a rock wall and at its foot, cross right over the stream. After that climb a steep, rugged rock rib and gully to the upper end of the steep step. Now go up less steep slopes to the moraine between Glacier de Planpancieux (west) and Glacier des Grandes Jorasses (east). Climb the moraine ridge and higher up go left and over a slabby step (II, chains, ladders) obliquely up to the *Grandes Jorasses Hut*, hung on the rocks above the Glacier de Planpincieux (*Rifugio Boccalatte*, 2804m, CAI Torino, 30 B, managed from mid-July to the end of August, ask in valley about current condition).

Summit climb: From the hut go up over debris and snow to the rock ridge which separates Glacier Planpincieux and the Glacier des Grandes Jorasses. Ascend snow on the left (north) under these rocks (on the eastern edge of the Glacier de Planpincieux). From the upper end of the rock ridge, keeping somewhat left (north) go up the very crevassed glacier, for about 300m to the lower end of the Rocher du Reposir (1½ hrs from the hut) a spur of Pointe Hélène. Climb the ridge on good holds (II and some III), usually exactly on its knife-edge, to its upper end (3 hrs from the hut). Traverse the steep glacier arm to the right (often threatened by avalanches in new snow or rotten afternoon snow) to the broad rock rib which descends from Pointe Whymper. Climb this, keeping left of the wildly disrupted Jorasses Glacier, up a sort of gully until one can traverse right into the flat glacier trough. Traverse swiftly eastwards (ice cliffs above and ice debris in the trough emphasise the urgency).

Move up the snow slope right of the ice cliffs and finally gain the ridge (keeping a respectful distance from the cornices overhanging to the right!) which leads directly to the summit of Pointe Walker.

(After crossing the glacier arm, one can also continue directly up the rib to Pointe Whymper and from there reach the highest point by the summit ridge. Even when the rock is dry this way is more difficult but takes about the same time. It is objectively safer and easier to find and for that reason is certainly a better way for the descent.)

View: The view to the west, over the adjacent summits of the crest and its continuation with Dôme de Rochefort and Dent du Géant, is dominated by Mont Blanc. The Chamonix Aiguilles are stretched out to the north-west with the Aiguille Verte and its satellites further to the right. To the north-east are the distinctly lower Petites Jorasses and Aiguille de Leschaux, east of them the portly mass of Mont Gruevetta, and behind that Mont Dolent and in the far distance the Grand Combin and the rest of the Pennine peaks. To the south the view extends over the foothills to the Po plain, and to the south-west to the Gran Paradiso.

Adjacent peaks: On the continuation of the ridge westwards stand **Pointe Whymper (4184m)**, **Pointe Croz (4101m)**, **Pointe Hélène (4045m)**, **Pointe Marguerite (4065m)** and **Pointe Young (3996m)**. These very prominent elevations can be traversed one after the other to or from the Col des Jorasses (D, in part IV, 6-8 hrs, the principal difficulties being between the Col and Pointe Marguerite).

Other worthwhile routes: *North-East or Hirondelles Ridge* (D+, with one pitch of V and several of IV, 750mH, 6-10 hrs from Col des Hirondelles).

South-East or Tronchey Ridge (TD, sustained at IV with several pitches of V in the upper part, 1600m long plus 1100mH).

North Pillar of Pointe Walker or Walker Spur (ED, VI, V+ and V, seldom less difficult than IV, in part mixed, ice to 55°-60°, mighty and splendid, predominantly good rock, objectively safe apart from some stone-fall danger on the approach slopes. In bad weather it quickly becomes a battle for survival. In good conditions it is often overcrowded, 1200mH, climbing distance about 2000m, in good conditions 14-18 hrs from the foot of the face).

190

Grandes Jorasses, Aiguille de Rochefort and Dent du Géant from the west.

North Buttress of Pointe Croz or Croz Spur (TD+, pitches of
V+ but mostly IV and III, mixed, ice to 60°, direct variation also
VI; 1100mH, 13-16 hrs from foot of face).
East Face (ED, sections of VI and V with pitches of A1, on
compact rock, 12-14 hrs from the Col des Hirondelles).
Guidebook: Mont Blanc Massif, Vol 1 (The Alpine Club, 1990).

191

Dôme de Rochefort, 4015m – Aiguille de Rochefort, 4001m

One of the most elegant snow ridges in the Alps, mostly narrow and exposed. Impressively decorated with the scroll work of seemingly playful cornices, and offering a range of fascinating views. The first ascent of the Aiguille de Rochefort was made in 1873, that of the Dôme de Rochefort eight years later, both by J. Eccles with the local Chamonix guides Michel-Clement and Alphonse Payot.

The ascent was made via the very crevassed Mont Mallet Glacier up the rather monotonous North Face. Today's normal route, a traverse along the West Ridge from the Dent du Géant, was first carried out in 1900 by E. Allegra with Laurent Croux, Pierre Dayné and Alexis Brocherel (in descent from the Aiguille), and in ascent with the continuation to the Dôme de Rochefort by Karl Blodig and M. Horten in 1903. Today, in settled weather and good conditions, it is a popular climb.

Difficulties: AD. Snow or ice to 50°, with some climbing to II and I.

Effort: The climb to the Torino Hut involves a mere 50mH from the téléphérique station or, on foot, a punishing 2000mH up a dilapidated path. The summit climb to Aiguille is 1050mH (4-6 hrs from the Torino Hut), to Dôme a further 250mH (2 hrs from the Aiguille). As the ridge is level the return takes about the same time.

Dangers: On the Glacier du Géant there are some open crevasses. On the ridge there are many cornices, in some sections overlapping. The worn track doesn't always take the safest line and constant judgement is required to assess its safety. Do not be misled by the aesthetically pleasing photographs in the well-known coffee-table books, which ignore all the rules about respecting fracture lines.

Pleasures: To climb this ridge in the morning sun is one of life's perfect experiences. In a pristine (untracked) state it looks like a piece of scenery shortly after the creation of the world.

Dent du Géant and Rochefort Ridge from the Aiguille de Rochefort.

Maps, sketches and travel: See Grandes Jorasses.

Hut climb: The horrible concrete stairs up the tunnel from the téléphérique station to the *Torino Hut* (3371m, CAI Torino & Aosta, 170 B, hotel and self-service restaurant from May to the end of September, Tel. 0165-84 22 47, from France 193 91-84 22 47). If one avoids an overnight stay one can start – at an unfavourably late hour – from the Pointe Helbronner, 3462m.

Summit Route by the Rochefort Ridge: From the hut cross to the Col du Géant (3365m, crevasses) and head north-eastwards round the rock spur of the Aiguilles Marbrées into the wide snow basin under the Col de Rochefort. Past this col and continue in the same direction up to the base of the prominent Aiguille du Géant. First of all, ascend on the left of a small snow couloir on the easy rocks to an adjacent ridge with a gendarme. From this, move across and climb on the right of the couloir, up to the broad main ridge. Move up the ridge, turning a gendarme on the right (east), to gain the Salle á Manger (breakfast place) below the South Face of the Dent du Géant (2-3 hrs from the hut).

Before reaching this, turn right and, staying on the narrow ridge (or, less promising, on the right below on the rock), cross the intermediate summit P.3933 and descend steeply on the other side. Continue along the sharp snow ridge to the rocky summit block of the **Aiguille de Rochefort**. Traverse right to a not very prominent gully. Climb this – steeply and on somewhat unstable rock, but with good holds – to gain the summit.

Make a rapid descent to the north-east to the broad saddle south-east of Mont Mallet (3989m) and go over a snow top. After that, pass the Doigt de Rochefort on the left (north-west) and keeping on the ridge reach the rocky summit block and gain the **Dôme de Rochefort**.

View: To the west the Dent du Géant, passed on the ascent, dominates the scene, and behind it is Mont Blanc. To the east is the adjacent Grandes Jorasses. The Chamonix Aiguilles are to the north-west and opposite them, on the other side of the Mer de Glace, the Drus and the Aiguille Verte. In the foreground, looking north-east the pinnacled ridge of the Périades descends to the Leschaux Glacier.

Adjacent peaks: Mont Mallet (3989m) can be easily incorporated into the expedition by an ascent from the saddle behind the Aiguille (III), and offers a fantastic view down to the Mer de Glace. The Calotte de Rochefort (3974m), east of the Dôme, is climbed by those who link up the Rochefort Ridge to a Grandes Jorasses traverse.

Other worthwhile routes: *North Face* (PD, dependent on the glacier conditions, preferably done in descent, so that one can abseil over the problematical bergschrund (possibly taking a wooden stake).

Ridge traverse to the Grandes Jorasses (D, a long, large-scale mixed route, with sections of IV; Col du Géant to Col des Jorasses/Canzio Bivouac 6-7 hrs, continuation to Pointe Walker 6-8 hrs, descent to Col des Hirondelles 5-6 hrs, only recommended in really settled weather).

Dent du Géant, 4013m

The Giant's Tooth. Anyone who is unfamiliar with this peak will recognise it immediately. It is a steep rock obelisk rising in a perfect position at the end of the knife-edged Rochefort Ridge. On the final section to the summit the climbing is impressively exposed giving this ascent a very exciting quality.

The Dent du Geant's history is characterised by acts of violence. After the failure of such notable climbers as Alexander Burgener, A.F. Mummery and others, rockets were used to shoot a rope over the summit as a climbing aid (which luckily miscarried). The first ascent was made in 1882, after eleven years of trying, in a more conventional way, albeit with massive use of artificial aids. Firstly the fore-summit (Pointe Sella, 4009m) was reached by Alessandro, Alfonso, Corradino and Gaudenzio Sella with Jean-Joseph, Baptiste and Daniel Maquignaz. Some weeks later the higher north-east summit (Pointe Graham, 4013m) was gained by Alphonse Payot and Auguste Cupelin with W.W. Graham. The first ascent of the Dent du Géant 'by fair means' was made in 1900 by the Austrians Heinrich Pfannl, Thomas Maischberger and Franz Zimmer who made an aid-free ascent by the 'usually iced' north edge. In 1935, the short but steep South Face, was climbed with many pitons, by H. Burggasser and R. Leitz in 1935.

Difficulties: AD. Climbing to III and with aid (strenuous and ungainly) from thick fixed ropes which is difficult if the ropes are iced up. It is worth taking some tape slings for belaying on the ropes and their huge anchor pegs.

Effort: Ascent to the Salle á Manger 550mH (2-3 hrs), summit block 180mH (1 hr).

Dangers: Objectively a very safe route, but beware of storms.

Pleasures: The pleasures would be untrammelled if the junk of the fixed ropes were dismantled and one could just enjoy the excellent rock.

Maps, travel, hut climb: See Aiguille de Rochefort.
Summit climb by the South-West Face: From the Torino Hut
follow the Aiguille de Rochefort route to the Salle á Manger.
Descend a little and traverse mixed ground to the left to the
south-west edge. On a detached slab move left to the edge and
up it a few metres to a piton. Then traverse 10m left to a shallow
gully (peg). Up this 30m to a terrace. Climb the beautiful gold-
brown slabs above ('Plaque Burgener'), which are disfigured
by thick hemp ropes. These lead to a good stance on the left
(west) edge. Now traverse right and climb two chimneys (peg,
ropes). Continue up walls and polished steps, always following
the sweat, scratches and hemp to the fore-summit (Pointe
Sella). Make an exposed descent north-west down a sort of
chimney into the notch and up a crack to the main summit
(Pointe Graham; Madonna).
View: On all sides this is extraordinarily impressive, like looking
from a balloon gondola. The Rochefort Ridge is close below.
There is a wide vista across the Glacier du Géant and Vallée
Blanche to the rock spurs of Mont Blanc du Tacul and beyond
them the overpowering bulk of Mont Blanc – all towering
high above.

Other worthwhile routes: *North Edge and North-West Face*
(D, IV and III, 280mH, 3 hrs from start of climb).
South Face (TD, keeping right V and A1, at least VI if climbed
free, 160mH, 3 hrs).
Guidebook: Mont Blanc Range, Vol 3 (The Alpine Club, 1976).

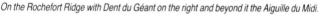

On the Rochefort Ridge with Dent du Géant on the right and beyond it the Aiguille du Midi.

The highest mountain in the Alps is – like the second highest, Monte Rosa – a range in itself. The ridges radiating from the summit carry proud mountain forms which only through their proximity to the monarch are made satellites. Those who wish to climb them should have no illusions about their immense scale and height, a factor reinforced by the absence of easy escape routes should the weather threaten.

Mont Blanc du Tacul, 4248m

A broad snow trapezium, Mont Blanc du Tacul forms the lowest step of a gigantic staircase to the summit of the Alps. One can admire it, yet, because of the milling crowds and swarming throng also loath it. The terrace of the Aiguille du Midi is full to bursting with people who having packed the cablecars to come up and then hang around for hours, without going out, waiting for the journey down again. Heretical thoughts come to one here and still more on the way over the glacier under the buzz of the gondolas of the connecting téléphérique to Pointe Helbronner which has been hit twice by jet fighters. This is an outrageous intrusion into the heart of what is soon to become the Mont Blanc International Nature Park and should be removed without trace as soon as possible.

The first ascent, generally recorded as 8 August, 1855, (Hudson, Kennedy and party) but a note in *The Alps in 1864* (1939 edition) states that, a week earlier, a Courmayeur party, with J.H. Ramsey, crossed the mountain *en route* on the way to Mont Blanc and that members of this group had been on this route a year earlier.

Amongst the many fine climbs on its eastern cliffs, the beautiful route along the South-East pinnacled Diable Ridge leading from the Grand Capucin to the summit was first climbed in 1928 by Armand Charlet and Georges Cachat with the Americans Miriam O'Brien and, her husband-to-be, Robert Underhill. The

Gervasutti Couloir (55°) on the North-East Face was first climbed in 1929 by the Italians D. Filipi, Piero Ghiglione and Francesco Ravelli, and more directly in 1934 by Giusto Gervasutti and Renato Chabod. In 1936 Gabriele Boccalatte and Nina Pietrasanta managed (in one day!) the first ascent of the longest buttress. In the struggle for the harder, neighbouring buttress, the leading Italian alpine climber, Giusto Gervasutti, fell to his death while abseiling during a retreat forced by bad weather. When his compatriots P. Fornelli and G. Mauro completed the route in 1951, they found his ice-axe and named the buttress after him. The lower, ice-encrusted (70°), rock triangle of the North Face was climbed in 1963 by André Contamine and Pierre Mazeaud. The rapid development of ice technique in the early seventies allowed the ascent of the almost vertical (400m) 'Supercouloir', climbed in 1973 in three days by Patrick Gabarrou and Jean-Marc Boivin.

Difficulties: PD. A glacier ascent with snow or ice to 40°.

Effort: Using the almost irresistible téléphérique to the Aiguille du Midi, the approach consists of merely a 300mH descent to the Col du Midi and then a 730mH ascent (3 hrs).

Dangers: The lower part of the glacier is threatened by infrequent but unpredicable sérac avalanches. The face is also prone to avalanche after new snow. Rope up at all times on the glacier, even if many people don't. Time and again this catches audacious climbers making ascents at the end of the season. In bad visibility navigation can be difficult particularly on the Col du Midi.

Pleasures: Impressive glacier scenery.

Maps and travel: See Aiguille Verte and Mont Blanc.

Hut climb: This is a descent because the téléphérique distorts the situation. The Cosmiques Hut which used to stand on the Col du Midi was burned down, is nevertheless rebuilt and should be reopened again in 1991 with 120 B. Bivouacing in the Aiguille du Midi station (3800m) is persistently refused.

The North-West Face of Mont Blanc du Tacul from the Chamonix valley with Col du Midi on the left.

Summit climb by the North-West Face: From the station, tramp through the tunnel and move out on to the slippery and unnervingly exposed East Ridge. Descend this until it becomes flatter and then head south down to the level Col du Midi (3532m).

Go up the slopes to the west of the steep rock and ice triangle of the North Face, over usually snow-clogged bergschrunds (later in the season they often yawn hungrily) and, keeping right, climb steeply upwards to the snow shoulder (Epaule du Mont Blanc du Tacul, c.4060m). Now move left (east) over the broad ridge to the summit.

View: To the north is the much ravaged Aiguille du Midi, teeming with people and reminiscent of a bee-hive. To the south-west are the steep glacier flanks of Mont Maudit, the next step in the gigantic staircase to Mont Blanc. To the east across the Glacier du Geant, the Dent du Géant and Grandes Jorasses catch the eye. And to the south-east beyond the pinnacles of the Diable Ridge is the Tour Ronde.

Adjacent peaks: The **East Summit (4247m)** is reached from the 1m higher West Summit with a short descent. By comparison, the most imposing towers further down the Diable Ridge, the **Isolée (Pointe Blanchard, 4114m), Pointe Carmen (4109m), Pointe Médiane (4097m), Pointe Chaubert (4074m)** and **Corne du Diable (4064m)**, can only be reached during the sporting ascent of the Diable Ridge, making them among the most innaccessible 4000m tops of the Alps. The same is correspondingly true for the difficult-to-access towers **Tour Rouge (c.4100m)** on the Gervasutti Pillar, as well as **P.4067** and **P.4027** on the steep face south of that.

Other worthwhile routes: *South-East Ridge or Arête du Diable* (D+, mixed climbing to V, mostly IV+ and IV; long, classic route on excellent rock with the principal difficulties at great height; 8-12 hrs from the Torino Hut).

Central Spur or Boccalatte Pillar (D+, in good conditions on the easiest line V, IV and III, but in snow and ice it soon becomes more difficult, 800mH, 5-8 hrs from foot of face).

Gervasutti Pillar (ED, VI and V with pitches of A1. A fine climb on excellent rock with escape possibilities higher up, 800mH, 8-12 hrs from foot of face).

Guidebook: Mont Blanc Massif, Vol 1 (The Alpine Club, 1990).

Mont Blanc du Tacul (left) and Mont Maudit (centre) from the Col du Midi.

Mont Maudit, 4465m

The accursed mountain. It lies halfway to the highest dome of the white mountain, far away from all easily accessible places. It can quickly become a killer in a sudden change of weather, but anyone who climbs it on a good day enjoys a wonderful experience on one of the highest and sharpest ice-clad pinnacles of the alps.

Mont Maudit was first climbed in 1878 by the Bernese Oberlanders Johann Jaun and Johann von Bergen with W.E. Davidson and H. Seymour Hoare. The first ascent of the fabulously beautiful South-East or Frontier Ridge was made in 1887 by the Swiss guides Alexander Burgener and Joseph Furrer, with their compatriot Moritz von Kuffner and a porter, in a three-day struggle. The difficult, mixed South-East Face was overcome in 1929 by Renato Chabod, Amilcare Crétier and L. Binel.

Mont Maudit is usually climbed with Mont Blanc du Tacul in the course of a traverse of Mont Blanc. Anyone who begins one of the more difficult climbs, should bear in mind that the descent to the Col du Midi is long and, in bad visibility, very hard to find.

Difficulties: PD. A glacier climb, with steep snow to 50°, which on account of its length and height should not be underestimated. Later in the season ascents from the north can become impossible through the opening of big bergschrunds. Then the only technically easy route is an ascent from Mont Blanc.

Effort: On setting out from the Aiguille du Midi 300mH descent and almost 1000mH ascent (6-8 hrs).

Dangers: Doing this climb from Aiguille du Midi can cause problems if one has not properly acclimatised. It is impossible to move fast as a late return in beautiful weather will be on soft snow with crampons balling-up. There may also be avalanche danger on both the North Face of Mont Maudit and the North-West Face of Mont Blanc du Tacul, particularly after new snow. The principal dangers of the climb lie in the weather. The summit area is very exposed to storms. The route-finding difficulties at such times are compounded by the fact that the compass does not work reliably on this mountain because of minerals present in the rock. For that reason, precise preparation through intensive memorization of map and photographs is important. In thoroughly bad weather, waiting for an improvement in a snow hole is the best life-saver, this nevertheless pre-supposes ample provisions and fuel as well as the best clothing.

Pleasures: In good weather, an experience that one has to share with all sorts of other people – whether one wants to or not.

Maps, travel and approach: See Aiguille Verte and Mont Blanc du Tacul.

Summit route by the North Face: Take the Mont Blanc du Tacul route as far as the Epaule of Mont Blanc du Tacul. Now go south, descending slightly into the extensive saddle of the Col du Maudit (4035m). Traverse right (west) out of this on a glacier terrace, under some séracs and then, traversing steadily right, climb across the steep face.

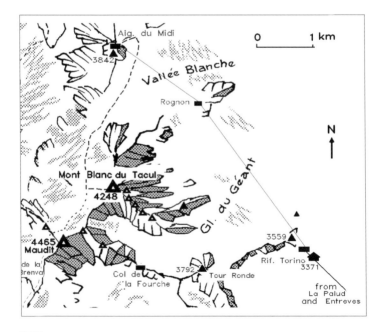

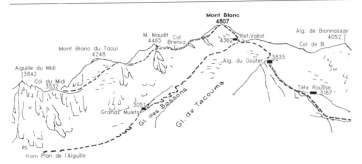

Cross the (sometimes large) bergschrund and continue right, across a very steep slope to the inconspicuous saddle of the Col du Mont Maudit (P.4345, here there is usually a wooden stake for belaying and abseiling).

Now follow the North-West Ridge with easy climbing (I) or traverse in a wide arc across and up the snow of the West Face to the bold rock tooth of the summit block.

On the traverse of Mont Blanc one descends north-eastwards from Mont Blanc over the broad slope, passing right of two rock outcrops, to a flatter slope (keep your distance from the cornices on the right over the Brenva Face!). Follow a spur descending to the left over the steep Mur de la Côte and go down to the Col de la Brenva (4303m, beware of cornices on the right!). Head north on the broad ridge (cornices!) over P.4361 and P.4369 to the saddle P.4342. Then go north-west up the steep but easy slope to the summit (2-3 hrs from the summit of Mont Blanc; for the rest of the way to Col du Midi allow a further 3-4 hrs). It is best to carry a wooden stake to cross the bergschrund below the Col du Mont Maudit.

View: To the west it is dominated by Mont Blanc. To the north are the huge glaciers that this massif debouches. To the east, behind Mont Blanc du Tacul, there extends a wide selection of high peaks, among which the Jorasses are especially conspicuous. To the south are the exciting views down across the Brenva Face.

Adjacent peaks: On the frontier ridge which first falls north-eastwards rises the **North-East Summit (4336m)** as a stylish snow ridge. On the ridge descending south-east from there to the Col de la Fourche, the gendarme **Pointe Androsace (4107m)** is conspicuous.

Mont Maudit from the south-east (from the Tour Ronde).

Other worthwhile routes: *South-East or Frontier Ridge* (D, climbing to IV and III, mixed, large-scale classic route at great height, along an extensive, narrow ridge, in part corniced, snow on long stretches at 45°, sometimes steeper; from the Col de la Fourche 800mH over 1.6km length of ridge, 4-8 hrs).

South-East Face (D+, a large-scale, mixed climb with climbing in places to IV and often harsh ice passages; 700mH, 7-10 hrs from the foot of the face).

Guidebook: Mont Blanc Massif, Vol 1 (The Alpine Club, 1990).

Mont Blanc, 4807m

The glittering dome high above in the deep blue sky, the monarch, the highest mountain in the Alps, in a word *the* summit in this part of the world. A symbol of scale and height, and a 'shy romanticism hiding behind flippant maxims'.

Just over 200 years ago, alpinism was founded with the first ascent of this peak. The reward of 20 gold thalers offered by the Geneva scientist Horace Bénédict De Saussure motivated the crystal hunter Jacques Balmat and the doctor Michel-Gabriel Paccard, who made the historical ascent on 8 August 1786. They took a route up the Rochers Rouges and the north-east slope. A year later De Saussure himself could enthuse on the summit over the sky's depth of blue and his own quick silver barometer, lugged up by a porter, which sank so 'magnificently low'.

The superlatives are certainly justified. Especially since the mountain offers an abundance of fantastic, bewitchingly beautiful climbs of all grades of difficulty. People from all over the world attempt the ascent. When *le grand beau temps* breaks out hundreds are underway to that snow top adorned by innumerable crampon holes – and yellow patches – under the criss-cross of the jet trails in the sky above. But not all who start out so enthusiastically come away unharmed. These blameless pale slopes have seen innumerable dramas. Time and again sudden storms bring tragedy through scatter-brained acts caused by the exhaustion triggered by the unaccustomed height and cold. They die of hypothermia, loss of direction in mist and driving snow, delirium, frostbite, crevasse falls and who knows what else – the annual death toll comes to almost three figures. Today the rescue helicopters of the Gendarmerie des Hautes Montagnes, weather permitting, dextrously and routinely collect up the accident victims and thus many survive who earlier would have died of exposure.

Some further high points of the development history of the mountain are still to be mentioned: in 1808 the peasant Marie Paradis from Chamonix was the first woman on the summit. About 1840 the ascent from Grands Mulets over Grand Plateau and Bosses Ridge was first carried out by Marie Couttet and company. In 1861 Melchior Anderegg, J.J. Bennen and Peter

Perren with Leslie Stephen and F.F. Tuckett climbed today's ordinary route over the Aiguille du Goûter and Bosses Ridge. Already by 1865 the mighty Brenva Spur was climbed by J. and M. Anderegg with G.S. Matthews, A.W. Moore and Frank and Horace Walker (father and son). In 1872 Jean-Antoine Carrel and J. Fischer with T.S. Kennedy made the first route up the mighty South-West Face. Today's usual ordinary route from the Italian side was found in 1890 by L. and J. Bonin and Achille Ratti (later Pope Pius XI) with J. Gadin and A. Proment. The first traverse of the Peuterey Ridge was carried out in 1893 by Emile Rey, Christian Klucker and César Ollier with the German Paul Güssfeldt (about whom the great Klucker in his memoirs expressed himself not at all flatteringly). In 1901 the Brouillard Ridge with north-west approach fell to G.B. and G.F. Gugliermina with Joseph Brocherel, and was climbed direct from Mont Brouillard on 9 August 1911 by Joseph Knubel with G.W. Young, H.O. Jones and K. Blodig (by which ascent Blodig secured the 'final victory' in the race for all the peaks at that time declared to be independent 4000ers). The Innominata Ridge was conquered in 1919 by Adolphe and Henri Rey as well as Adolf Aufdenblatten with S.L. Courtauld and E.G. Oliver.

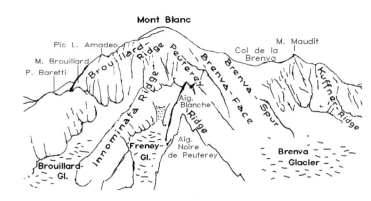

Mont Blanc from the south.

In 1927 T. Graham Brown and F.S. Smythe made the direct route (guideless) on the imposing Brenva Face by the Red Sentinel and a year later also the further left and still more difficult Route Major to the highest saddle in the Alps. The first face climb on the Frêney side was made in 1940 by Giusto Gervasutti and P. Bollini di Predosa by their ascent of the right-hand Frêney Pillar. Revelling in bivouacs, Walter Bonatti and Andrea Oggioni immortalized themselves in 1959 with the far left Pilier Rouge on the Pic Luigi Amedeo. The most exacting of the well-known Mont Blanc climbs is the Central Pillar of Frêney which was first climbed in 1961 by Chris Bonington, Don Whillans, Ian Clough and Jan Djugloz, a month after the tragic deaths of four fine climbers during the attempt led by Walter Bonatti and Pierre Mazeaud.

The customary ordinary route is that over the Aiguille du Goûter. Only a few climbers ascend from the far lower Grands Mulets Hut. The same is true of the route from the Italian side. From the Col du Dôme onwards, all three routes finish up the Bosses Ridge to the highest point.

Difficulties: On the *Aiguille du Goûter Route* (PD), on the rock rib pitches of II, otherwise only snow plodding. On the Bosses Ridge (40°), neat crampon work is required while at the same time one fights dizziness and headaches and gasps for air.

The Grands Mulets Route (PD–) is twice as long, but involves only normal glacier work with many crevasses and a constantly changing line. The route from the Gonella Hut (PD+) also utilizes a long, disrupted glacier (an alternative non-glacier variation over the Aiguilles Grises is PD with mixed climbing to II). In all these cases the easy grades disguise the overall seriousness of an ascent of such a high mountain which must never be taken lightly.

Effort: From the rack railway to the Tête Rousse Hut 800mH (2-3 hrs), from there to the Goûter Hut 700mH (2-3 hrs), and to the summit a further 1050mH (4-5 hrs). From the téléphérique station Plan de l'Aiguille to the Grands Mulets Hut 800mH (3 hrs), from there 1776mH (6-7 hrs) to the summit. From Lac Combal in the Val Veni 1050mH (4 hrs) to the Gonella Hut, from there 1736mH (7-8 hrs) to the summit.

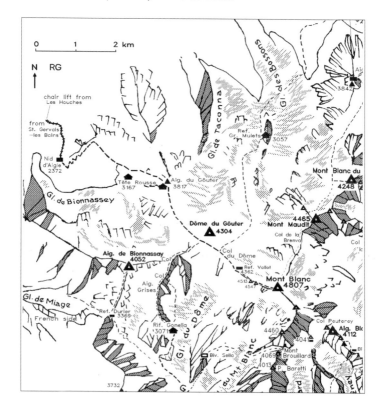

Dangers: The Goûter Hut climb is menaced by stone-fall (especially if one crosses the big couloir above the Tête Rousse Hut in order to ascend the technically easier rock rib south of that) and the route is more exposed to the wind, as compensation there are few crevasses. The Grands Mulets route is occasionally exciting on account of crevasses, especially if one of the helpfully placed ladders is missing. The route-finding presents no difficulties in good weather but quickly becomes desperate in a snow storm. The Italian route has a likewise disrupted glacier. It is well to note that the often swift weather changes on Mont Blanc can transform the peaceful, sunny ordinary routes full of people into a hostile maelstrom within a short time. The Vallot Hut is merely a survival box for emergencies and is a miserable, neglected thing. Nevertheless, it is as well to make a scrupulous note of its position as it could be a life-saver in poor weather. People have frozen to death because they had been unable to find it in a snow storm.

Apart from the objective dangers, it is essential, nevertheless, to be sure that one's fitness and acclimatization are sufficient for the task and, if in serious doubt, to turn back at the right time. Thus, with luck, the helicopter pilots won't have to take off yet again ...

Pleasures: If all goes to plan, then the hours on the roof of the Alps are an unforgettable experience in various respects. As a precaution against disappointment in good weather, prepare yourself for a frightful crowd, with awkward passing manouevres on the narrow Bosses Ridge, and with many inconsiderate people. If you plan this in as an expectation beforehand, the reality may just be bearable.

Maps: IGN carte touristique 1:25,000, 1 Chamonix-Mont Blanc and 2 St Gervais les Bains.

Travel: By rail or car to *Chamonix* (1030m, 40km from Martigny, 86km from Geneva, 59km from Aosta; a tourist resort and alpinists' Mecca; for further details, see Aiguille Verte); from there 8km to *Les Houches* (1000m).

Hut climb: From Les Houches by téléphérique up to Bellevue (1790m, station on the tramway from St Gervais les Bains).

Take the tramway to the terminus Nid d'Aigle (2386m). Go south on the path for 200m, then head left (east) in zig-zags under a rocky step up into a scree hollow. At a small hut, go right (south-east) over debris to the ridge which leads up in the direction of the Aiguille du Goûter. On a small plateau on the right is the *Tête Rousse Hut* (3167m, 60 B, managed from June to September, Tel. 50-58 24 97; if one wants to climb directly to the Aiguille du Goûter, one need not cross over). Cross the small Tête Rousse Glacier to the rock rib which runs left (north) of a big couloir. Keeping on this rib climb straight up to the north summit of the Aiguille du Goûter. Follow the linking ridge to the *Goûter Hut* placed on the west side close under the summit (3817m, CAF Paris & Chamonix, 100 B, managed from the end of June to end of September, in summer generally hope-lessly overcrowded, winter room with 16 B always open, Tel. 50-54 40 93, advance booking advisable).

Summit climb from Aiguille du Goûter: From the Goûter Hut head south, then south-east along the broad snow ridge to the Dôme du Goûter. Cross the summit (4303m) or turn it on the south, make a slight descent to the Col du Dôme (4240m). Continue in the same direction, up the steepening slope. Pass the *Vallot Hut*, standing on a rock on the left (4362m, 8 B; squalid). Climb the soon narrowing and steepening ridge

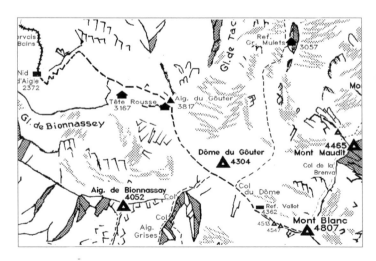

(usually a broad and deep track) to two snowy ridge humps (Grande Bosse 4513m and Petite Bosse 4547m) and after that go along a sharp snow ridge passing the rocks of La Tournette (4677m) on the right, and then heading east, to the last top (4740m) and 300m beyond that, the summit.

View: All the surrounding summits are dwarfed by Mont Blanc's height. To the south are Gran Paradiso and the Haut Dauphiné.

On the summit of Mont Blanc.

There is a distant view to the Pennine peaks in the east. In all directions are dominating views, as Edward Whymper described when commenting on the disappointment of purely panoramic views. 'That seen from Mont Blanc itself is notoriously unsatisfactory... There is nothing to look up to; all is below; there is no one point for the eye to rest upon. The man who is there is somewhat in the position of one who has attained all that he desires – he has nothing to aspire to; his position must needs be unsatisfactory.' Whymper was right. If one only climbs Mont Blanc for the view then there will be a sense of anti-climax, for the view is like that from an aircraft.

Summit climb via Grands Mulets: From Chamonix take the Midi téléphérique to the halfway station Plan de l'Aiguille. From there take the marked path to the south to the Glacier des Pélerins. The bare tongue of this is crossed at about 2400m.

Summit climb via Grands Mulets: From Chamonix take the Midi téléphérique to the halfway station Plan de l'Aiguille. From there take the marked path to the south to the Glacier des Pélerins. The bare tongue of this is crossed at about 2400m. Continue on a good path to the derelict téléphérique station 'Gare des Glaciers' (2414m). Ascend on the left side of the Glacier des Bossons, under a big couloir of the Aiguille du Midi (stone-fall danger) to gain the glacier. Traverse this to the south-west to the badly disrupted area of La Jonction (usually ladders over the most awkward crevasses). Now work southwards, going up over the crevassed snow slopes, first keeping right (west) of the rock island and then moving onto it where a path with an iron handrail leads up to the *Grands Mulets Hut* (3051m, private, 68 B, managed in spring and summer, Tel. 50-53 16 98).

From the hut, cross the glacier heading obliquely south-west in the direction of some rocks at the foot of the long north ridge of the Dôme du Goûter. Near the séracs of the Dôme, go left over a steep slope (the Petites Montées) to a flatter ramp-like section (Petit Plateau, 3650m, 2 hrs). Keeping well away from the séracs of the Dôme, climb this flat section. After that, go up a further steep slope. Higher up, after an especially big crevasse, bear right to the extensive snow-field of the Grand Plateau (3980m). Traverse this west-south-westwards and climb the seemingly endless slope to the Col du Dôme (6-7 hrs from the Grands Mulets Hut). Continue as for Goûter route (see above).

The Italian Route via the Gonella Hut: Start from the Val Veni from Cantine de la Visaille (1653m, bus from Courmayeur; cf. sketch to Aiguille Blanche and Goûter route). Take the path along the moraines on the northern bank of the Miage Glacier. Alternatively, from Lac Combal (1940m), further up the valley, take a path over the big moraine on the south side to reach the Miage Glacier. Ascend the middle of the glacier. Pass below the Dôme Glacier (2493m) on the right and go on to P.2530 at the foot of the southern spur of the Aiguilles Grise. Take a path on the right, 150m beyond P.2530, first up a scree couloir, then working steeply up east to cross a shoulder on the ridge to reach the Dôme Glacier side. Continue up and across, bending right, across couloirs and snow slopes to a rock spur which leads up to the Gonella Hut (3071m, CAI, 40 B, managed from mid-July to the end of August, Tel. 0165-893 69).

Summit Climb from the Dôme Glacier: Ascend near the western edge of the glacier, then move towards the centre (crevasses). Higher up take the left (west) arm of the glacier, cross the bergschrund and go left to the Col des Aiguilles Grises (3809m, 3 hrs, this point can also be reached by following the Aiguilles Grises ridge from the hut (PD), climbing over the first two towers, turning the third on the west side by descending somewhat and after that on the broad snow ridge over the summit of the Calotte des Aiguilles Grises, 3826m to the col, 4 hrs). Now continue northwards on the ridge. Turn a rock rise on the left and continue on the snow ridge to the shoulder (4003m) on the frontier ridge just above the Col de Bionnassay. Continue (northeast) up the often corniced ridge to a further shoulder (4153m, iron posts) and then on to the Dôme du Goûter (4303m) to join the Goûter route (see page 210).

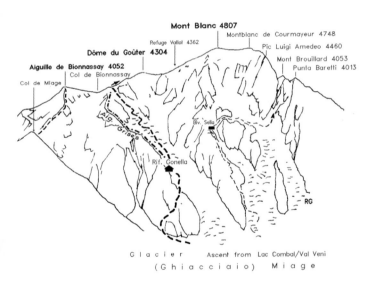

Adjacent peaks: Mont Blanc de Courmayeur (4748m) is the south-east summit 600m away beyond the rocky P.4741, La Tournette. The **Dôme du Goûter (4303m)** as well as **Grande Bosse (4513m)** and **Petite Bosse (4547m)** are traversed on the ascent from the Aiguille du Goûter. The more independent **Pic Luigi Amedeo (4469m)** is only reached on an ascent of the Brouillard Ridge. **Pic Eccles (4041m)** lies close to the Innominata

Bivouac Hut. The **Grande Chandelle (c.4600m)** is the rock tower at the top of the Central Frêney Pillar. The not very independent shoulder summit **Grand Pilier d'Angle (4243m)** is crossed when climbing the upper Peuterey Ridge.

Other worthwhile routes: *South-West Face* (PD, mixed and snow to 50°, 1400mH, 6-8 hrs from the dilapidated Quintino Sella Hut).

Brouillard Ridge (AD+, a classic ridge, in part on loose rock, to III+, 2200mH, 10-18 hrs from the Monzino Hut).

Innominata Ridge (D+, a classic, especially beautiful ridge, mixed, 1450mH, 12-17 hrs from the Monzino Hut, 7-10 hrs from the Eccles Bivouac Hut).

Traverse of Aiguille Blanche and Peuterey Ridge (D+, rock to IV–, over a long distance III and II, mixed, with snow or ice to 55°, 2500mH, 10-20 hrs from Monzino Hut).

Brenva Spur (AD to D, according to conditions, predominantly snow or ice to 50°, occasionally extreme at the exit, marvellous line, objectively safe, 900mH to exit, 1300mH to summit, 7-10 hrs from the Trident Hut).

The Brenva Face by the Sentinelle Rouge Route (D+, snow or ice to 55° and rock to III, ideal line direct to the main summit, but with danger of falling ice, 1200mH to exit, 1400mH to summit, 9-13 hrs from the Trident Hut).

The Brenva Face by the Route Major (TD, ice to 57°, rock to V and IV, mixed, great danger of falling ice, especially in the crossing of the Grand Couloir, 1000mH face, 1300mH to summit, about 11-16 hrs from the Trident Hut).

Right-Hand Frêney Pillar or Gervasutti Pillar (TD, rock to VI, and A1, mixed, 800mH, 8-12 hrs from the Col Peuterey).

Central Frêney Pillar (ED+, rock to VI and A3, mixed – at the end of the world and, given bad luck, delivered up to all the hells of sudden changes of weather, 15-25 hrs from Col Peuterey).

Guidebook: Mont Blanc Range, Vol 1 (The Alpine Club, 1990).

Mont Blanc from the Tour Ronde, showing the Brenva Face with the upper Peuterey Ridge and the Aiguille Blanche on the left, separated by the Col Peuterey.

Aiguille de Bionnassay, 4052m

As the stylish and picturesque western satellite of Mont Blanc, the Aiguille de Bionnassay displays to the Aiguille du Goûter opposite, its impressive North-West Face and North Wall. The first ascent of the peak was made in 1865 over the mighty hanging glacier of the North-West Face by Jean-Pierre Cachat and Michel-Clement Payot with E.N. Buxton, F.C. Grove and R.J.S. MacDonald. By comparison, from the Dôme du Goûter the East Ridge leads down to its summit with the South Ridge in profile on the left. This latter ridge is the easiest ascent route and was done for the first time in 1888 by Kaspar Maurer and Andreas Jaun with their client G. Gruber.

Difficulties: PD+. A mixed ridge climb with passages of II. The summit slope is steep snow 45°, there is also troublesome ice.

Effort: The ascent to the Durier Bivouac Hut from the north-west from Tresse is 2250mH (8 hrs), from the south-east from Lac Combal in the Val Veni 1700mH (5-7 hrs). Summit climb by the South Ridge 700mH (3-5 hrs). Continuation toward Mont Blanc by the East Ridge (AD, 150 mH, 1 hr to the Col de Bionnassay).

Dangers: A quite beautiful rough approach. On the ridges, beware of cornices.

Pleasures: A region protected from overcrowding by the sheer effort of getting there. All visitors should appreciate such rarity and leave things behind in good condition.

Maps: IGN carte touristique 1:25,000, 2 Mont Blanc-Trelatete. See also Mont Blanc sketches.

Travel: By rail to *St Gervais-les-Bains*, from there by bus through the Val Montjoie in the direction of Les Contamines 6km to Tresse (1050m). For the Italian side, see Mont Blanc.

Approach to the Durier Bivouac Hut: *From Tresse*, head eastwards through the village, then left (north) to the Torrent de Miage. Follow a path along the south-west bank (2 hrs) to the Miage chalets (1559m). Cross to the other side and follow an indistinct path up the valley. Climb the rock steps to the right of a waterfall climb. After that, climb steeper grass and rock slopes to the northern moraine of the Glacier de Miage. Follow the path along this, climbing laboriously over P.2566, and continue to a flat part of the glacier on the right. After turning the rocky foot of the South-West Face of the Aiguille de Tricot. Cross the glacier ascending to the east to the central rock rib descending from the Col de Miage. Cross the (often awkward) bergschrund at the earliest opportunity (far left), then climb the crumbling rib to the *Durier Bivouac Hut*, placed just under the col on the west (3349m, CAF St Gervais 8 B).

Approach *Lac Combal* by the Miage Glacier: Take the Gonella Hut route to P.2530. Continue along the south-west side of the glacier in the direction of the Col de Miage. Where the Bionnassay Glacier joins, climb north-west starting on the left and going up over a step to a steep snow-field. Go up this in direction of a snow hump (crevasses). Finally, move right towards rocks to gain the Col de Miage.

Summit climb by the South Ridge: From the Col de Miage take the snow ridge to a shoulder. Continue to a second snow shoulder with blocks and on to a notch behind it in front of a rock step. This can be climbed keeping just right of the edge and then by linking chimneys and ledges regain the ridge above. If this is verglassed it is possible to go up further right across the South-East Face, firstly keeping low along a snow ledge, passing below ribs and couloirs until a steep, right-slanting snow band and a funnel through a rock band allows the ridge to be regained (AD). This leads to a final steep snow slope and the summit.

East Ridge: From the Italian ordinary route to Mont Blanc (see page 213) descend to the Col de Bionnassay from P.4003. From there, an exciting, narrow snow and ice ridge decorated with cornices leads to the summit (1 hr). Alternatively this might be descended on a traverse to the Gouter Route (AD).

View: This is dominated by the nearby Mont Blanc and the Trélatete group to the south.

Other worthwhile routes: *West-North-West or Tricot Ridge* (PD, climbing to II, very long, 2250mH, 3.8km, 10 hrs from the Col de Tricot).
North-West Face (AD, a snow and ice climb, mostly 40°, but in places 55°, after new snow there is avalanche danger, 1050mH, 5-9 hrs from the Tête Rousse Hut).

Guidebook: Mont Blanc Range, Vol. 1 (The Alpine Club, 1990).

Mont Brouillard, 4053m – Punta Baretti, 4013m

On the south-west side of Mont Blanc are the gigantic glacier basins of the Miage and Brouillard Glaciers, which can only be linked by the difficult Col Emile Rey at the foot of the mighty Brouillard Ridge. These two ridge tops are lost in this 'Himalaya of the Alps', at the end of the world and only visited by people who are addicted to 4000m peak collecting or those who have a weakness for the last lonely corners of the continent.

Naturally they are also the sort of mountains whose independence has been exhaustively debated, as the col depth of the lower Punta Baretti is distinctly greater than that of the higher Mont Brouillard. There was also a dispute over the first ascent because the first climbers of the Punta Baretti – Martino Baretti and Jean Joseph Maquignaz in 1880 – gave inexact details about the traverse to Mont Brouillard. The critical 4000er collector Karl Blodig sharply observed that he, Oscar Eckenstein and A. Brocherel found no cairn on Mont Brouillard in 1906 and their ascent is now thought to be the first.

Difficulties: AD. Rock difficulties to II, mostly I and scrambling, mixed, snow or ice to 50° and disrupted glaciers.

Effort: From the west by the Sella Bivouac Hut 1400mH (5 hrs), summit climb 800mH (5 hrs).

Dangers: Many problems – crevasses, avalanche danger, stone-fall, falling ice and all the additional factors which go with remoteness.

Pleasures: Extreme remoteness.

Maps, travel, sketches: See Grandes Jorasses and Mont Blanc.

Hut approach: As for the Gonella Hut (see Mont Blanc) along the Miage Glacier to its junction with the Mont Blanc Glacier.

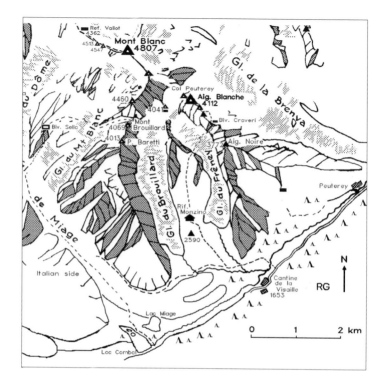

Turn the ice-fall on the left (orogr. right) close to the edge battling with crevasses and over the usually very complicated bergschrund to the first grassy rock gully of the ridge. Climb it over broken rocks following the tracks as far as one third height. Then go obliquely right over broken slopes to a rock wall which is climbed using a gully to gain the ridge. Climb this with easy scrambling, first of all to the remains of an old hut, then to the newer *Quintino Sella Bivouac Hut* (3371m, 15 B).

Summit climb by the West Couloir: Traverse the snow slopes eastwards. Cross three rounded ribs and three snow gullies and descend over the disrupted Mont Blanc glacier to the foot of the snow gully which descends from the Col Emile Rey. According to conditions, ascend this near the middle or on the right (south) bordering rocks up to the Col Emile Rey (4012m). Now go south on the ridge on easy mixed ground to the summit of Mont Brouillard (15-30 mins from the col).

To Punta Baretti from Mont Brouillard – descend the connecting ridge and climb up to Punta Baretti (1 hour), turning obstacles as necessary.

View: Mont Blanc's Brouillard Ridge rises immediately to the north blotting out all views in that direction. To the west is the Trélatete group, to the east the Peuterey Ridge and to the south the Gran Paradiso range. Below are huge glaciers riven with hungry crevasses.

Other routes: *South-West Ridge* (PD, pitches of II, seemingly endlessly long and boring, 2100mH from the Miage Glacier). *From the south-east* (AD, snow or ice to 50°, long glacier ascent using Eccles Bivouac Hut and with snow traverses and rock ribs to the Col Emile Rey, 1500mH, 6-9 hrs from the Monzino Hut).

Guidebook: Mont Blanc Range, Vol 1 (The Alpine Club, 1990).

The Brouillard Face of Mont Blanc. Mont Brouillard is on the left with Pic Luigi Amedeo and Mont Blanc de Courmayeur the other obvious summits. The peak on the right, in the middle distance, is the Punta Innominata.

Aiguille Blanche, 4112m

One of the most fascinating mountains in the Alps, with the elegant rock pillars on its south-western flank and equally well-sculpted ice ramparts on the north-east. Between them, the mighty Peuterey Ridge rises to the summit from Brèche Nord des Dames Anglaises.

The peak is generally climbed in the course of a traverse to Mont Blanc (when the need for speed means that only the south summit is crossed with the other two being turned). Anyone who embarks on this ascent must be very well prepared in terms of both fitness and experience for this is the most difficult independent 4000er in the Alps. The approaches are long and complicated, and threatened by both ice and stonefall and with plenty of scope for going astray. The mountain itself is big and complicated and when one has finally reached the narrow knife-edge of the summit ridge, the quickest way to safety involves either a further very long ascent, or a choice of complicated descents neither of which is without risk. This is not a place to get caught in bad weather.

The first ascent of the Aiguille Blanche de Peuterey was made in 1885 by Emile Rey, Ambros Supersaxo and Aloys Anthamatten with H. Seymour King, who climbed the North-West Ridge via the Col de Frêney and Col de Peuterey. The first traverse of the classic Peuterey Ridge with ascent up the Brenva flank was made in 1893 by Emile Rey, Christian Klucker and César Ollier with Paul Güssfeldt. Today's usual ridge route, using the Frêney Glacier approach, was found in 1928 by L. Obersteiner and K. Schreiner. The North Face was climbed in 1933 by Renato Chabod and Aimé Grivel. The South Face of the Punta Gugliermina fell in 1938 to the immortal Giusto Gervasutti and G. Boccalatte.

Difficulties: D+. Rock-climbing sustained at III and II with passages of IV, mixed, seldom easy, snow or ice to 50°. The principal difficulty lies, nevertheless, not in individual pitches, but rather in the length and the sustained and changing demands. For that reason, the ascent can only be recommended to fully fit, experienced climbers who should only set out in favourable conditions and when the weather is settled. Most will elect to complete the climb by crossing Mont Blanc.

The North Face of Aiguille Blanche seen from the Col de la Fourche.

Effort: Hut climb 1000mH (3 hrs), bivouac approach 1100mH (4-7 hrs), summit climb from there 700mH (5-6 hrs), continuation to Col Peuterey 150mH descent (2 hrs), descent by the Rochers Gruber and back to the Monzino Hut 1650mH descent and 150mH ascent (c.5-8 hrs) or, alternatively, a continuation to Mont Blanc involves another 850mH (5-10 hrs).

Dangers: Everything that can possibly be encountered in the high mountains – crevasses on the very disrupted glaciers are a particularly serious problem when retreating; stone-fall in the couloir to the Brèche Nord des Dames Anglaises, especially in 'good' conditions; loose rock on the rib on the South-East Face; hypothermia on the summit ridge in storm; avalanches on the Rochers Gruber in bad weather, etc. Anyone who embarks on this peak must be able to deal with all of these.

The principal problem remains the danger of being overtaken by bad weather with the consequent forced retreat. This will usually be down the Rochers Gruber, which is difficult, complicated and dangerous (with difficult ascent to the Col de l'Innominata) and must not be under-estimated. Abundant food and fuel can become life-saving. Two parties climbing together can give additional security by speeding the abseiling at the critical stages.

Pleasures: Aesthetically, in its entirety, highly enjoyable for those who can cope with this sort of demand.

Maps: IGN carte touristique 1:25,000, 2 Mont Blanc-Trélatete.

Travel: To *Courmayeur* (1230m) via the Val d'Aosta or from the north through the Mont Blanc tunnel. See also Grandes Jorasses and Mont Blanc sketches.

Hut climb: By bus or car along the Val Veni as far as Cantine de la Visaille (1653m). Cross the main stream to the Chalets de Frêney. From there, take the marked track over a gigantic scree fan and then, keeping left (west) of the stream descending from the Frêney Glacier, climb the rugged face with many bends. Finally take the climbing path with fixed wires etc. up three tiers of slabs to the saddle by the Aiguille du Châtelet and the *Monzino Hut* (2561m, Guides de Courmayeur, 60 B, managed from mid-June to the end of September, Tel. 0165-80 95 53).

Bivouac approach: From the hut go north-east under the walls of the Aiguille Croux, and ascend over debris and snow into the cirque in front of the Punta Innominata.

On the long rock rib of the south-east side of the Aiguille Blanche with the ice labyrinths of the Brenva Glacier far below.

From the snow of this cirque go right (east) over rocks and up a gully to the Col de l'Innominata (3205m, 2-3 hrs from the hut). On the other side, abseil down a steep gully and then descend to the Frêney Glacier. Take an adventurous route through the crevasse labyrinth to reach and climb the snow couloir descending from the Brèche Nord. If the bergschrund is impassable, or impassable, or there is acute danger of stone-fall, the Schneider Couloir, running parallel to the main couloir but well to the left, below the Punta Gugliermina, is less dangerous. Higher up take the left (north) branch, to the notch (3470m, obliquely left above is the *Craveri* or *Dames Anglaises Bivouac Hut*, 3490m.

Summit climb by the Peuterey Ridge: Above the notch, a steep rise bars the way ahead. Go left (west) and climb up and down on the wall of the rise, climb a short chimney and then, on shelves and ledges, cross some 40m (III and II) to a slabby, gully-like couloir. Climb the couloir (III) to the notch on an adjacent ridge, right of a thin pinnacle. On the right go up a sort of gully (III) for 10m to easy ground above the first steep rise. Up the ridge for a short way, then traverse right (Brenva side) over debris and snow to rubble ribs which are separated from one another by snow gullies. The third rib is the best, climb this directly, high above the criss-crossed Brenva Glacier, with occasional crumbling rock, until it ends at a notch on the main ridge (about 100m to the side and somewhat above the Punta Gugliermina). Ascend the ridge, then descend on the right to a prominent notch in front of a tower. Turn this airily on the left (IV). After that, go up to the ridge again and on this finally on a broad snow ridge to the south-east top (4107m, Pointe Seymour King).

On the other side, go down a short brittle gully to the narrow snow ridge. Traverse across on its knife-edge (very exposed) to the central summit (4112m, Pointe Güssfeldt) and continue to the North-West Summit (4104m, Pointe Jones). These two summits are often turned – the Central on the Brenva side, the North-West on the Frêney side – which can involve climbing on very hard ice.

View: An overwhelming aspect of the Frêney Face of Mont Blanc opposite, and on the right is the, apparently less fierce, Brenva Face. Otherwise, one has ample opportunity here to contemplate just how far and steeply the ground drops away everywhere and how one might best escape from such a place.

Descent: Head north down to a rocky shoulder. Go steeply down from a fixed abseil point on the North-West Face and, most conveniently, abseil 40m from the lowest rocks to clear the bergschrund and thence descend to the Col de Peuterey

On the traverse from the South-East Summit to the Central Summit (at the right edge of the picture) of Aiguille Blanche. Col Eccles and its approaches are above and left of the figure.

(3934m). Now one must decide whether to continue upwards to the summit of Mont Blanc or to go down.

The former is better. For the next stage there are two possibilities (both taking 2-4 hrs), on the left (west) of the ridge edge leading to the top of the Grand Pilier d'Angle – either traverse left a short distance until below where the ridge angles eases and

227

cross the bergschrund here (often awkward) before working right to regain the ridge; alternatively, make a longer (150m) traverse left before heading directly up a ramp of mixed climbing (stone-fall danger) to gain the ridge behind the Grand Pilier by a gendarme. After this climb the corniced ridge and finally up the steepening snow or ice face to the summit cornices of Mont Blanc de Courmayeur (very long and in bad weather quickly murderous).

In good conditions, a feasible descent is to cross over the Frêney Glacier and climb up to the Col Eccles and the bivouac box there, usually over-crowded in good weather. From there, descend to the Monzino Hut, down the abundantly crevassed Brouillard Glacier, possibly helped by tracks. This provides a good escape providing the col can be reached before the weather breaks but in new snow the Frêney basin quickly becomes avalanche prone.

Another way is the descent of the *Rochers Gruber*, a steep rognon between the Aiguille Blanche and the highest ice-fall of the Frêney Glacier. To start, descend from the col south-south-westwards to the beginning of a snow ridge (not easy to find in mist) and down this until it changes into a steep snow and rock rib. First descend on the left (east) near the rock rib on steep snow as far as a steep drop. Above the drop cross over to the rocks on the right. Now abseil, keeping right and using several small traverses to gain the lower Frêney Glacier. Descend the very crevassed slopes until under the Col de l'Innominata which is then gained up a steep gully (difficult). On the other side an easier descent leads down to the Monzino Hut. If a Rochers Gruber descent is thought too dangerous, digging a snow hole will buy time to consider the remaining options.

Adjacent peaks: Apart from the seldom climbed summit (4112m, Pointe Gussfeldt) there is also the North-West Summit (4104m, Pointe Jones) and the customarily climbed South Summit (4107m, Pointe Seymour King). To the south is the striking Punta Gugliermina (3893m).

Other worthwhile routes: *North Face* (TD, a pure ice face averaging 52° with some 55°, 800mH, 5-7 hrs for the face). Punta Gugliermina South Face (TD+, a rock climb sustained at V+ and V, with sections of VI and AI, 600mH, 11-16 hrs from Rifugio Monzino).

Guidebook: Mont Blanc Range, Vol 1 (The Alpine Club, 1990).

Books and Guides in English about the 4000m Peaks

All publishers based in London unless otherwise noted. G denotes guidebooks.

Brailsford, J. *The Écrins Massif* (G) Alpine Club, 1988.

Bonatti, W. *On the Heights* Hart Davis, 1964.

Clark, R.W. *The Early Alpine Guides* Phoenix House, 1950.

Clark, R.W. *The Victorian Mountaineers* Batsford, 1953.

Clark, R.W. *An Eccentric in the Alps* Museum Press, 1959.

Collomb, R.G. *Graians East* and *Bernina Alps* (G) West Col, Reading 1969/1976.

Collomb, R.G. *Pennine Alps* (G. 3 Vols). Alpine Club, 1974-79.

Collomb, R.G. *Bernese Alps* (G. 2 Vols). Alpine Club, 1979.

Daudet, A. *Tartarin on the Alps* Dent, 1885.

Gos, C. *Alpine Tragedy* Allen & Unwin, 1948.

Griffin, L. *Mont Blanc Range* (G. 2 Vols). Alpine Club, 1990-91.

Finch, G. *The Making of a Mountaineer* Arrowsmith, Bristol 1924.

Irvine, R.L.G. *The Romance of Mountaineering* Dent; Dutton, New York 1935.

Irvine, R.L.G. *The Alps* Batsford, 1938.

Klucker, C. *Adventures of an Alpine Guide* Murray, 1932.

Kugy, J. *Alpine Pilgrimage* Murray, 1934.

Moore, A.W. *The Alps in 1864* Blackwell, Oxford 1939.

Mummery, A.F. *My Climbs in the Alps and Caucasus* T. Fisher, Unwin, 1895.

Rébuffat, G. *The Mont Blanc Massif* Kaye and Ward; Oxford University Press, New York 1973.

Rey, G. *The Matterhorn* Blackwell, 1946.

Roch, A. *On Rock and Ice* A. and C. Black, 1947.

Smythe, F. *Climbs and Ski Runs* Blackwood, Edinburgh 1933.

Smythe, F. *A Camera in the Hills* Black, 1939.

Smythe, F. *Again Switzerland* Hodder & Stoughton, 1947.

Stephen, L. *The Playground of Europe* Longmans Green 1907.

Underhill, M. *Give Me the Hills* Methuen, 1956.

Whymper, E. *Scrambles Amongst the Alps* Murray, 1871.

Young, G.W. *On High Hills* Methuen; Dutton, New York 1927.

All Four Thousanders of the Alps by height

In bold type those customarily taken as independent, in ordinary print the neighbouring peaks (peaklets). On the right the height of the col to the next highest peak (as scale for the independence of the summit, in part estimated).

Height above lowest col

		Height above lowest col
1.	**Mont Blanc 4807m**	4600m
2.	Mont Blanc de Courmayeur 4748m	18m
3.	**Dufourspitze 4634m**	2165m
4.	Dufourspitze – E. ridge tower c.4630m	15m
5.	Monte Rosa Grenzgipfel 4618m	10m
6.	**Nordend 4609m**	94m
7.	Dufourspitze – western fore-summit c.4600m	10m
8.	Mont Blanc Frêney Gr.Chandelle c.4600m	20m
9.	**Zumsteinspitze 4563m**	111m
10.	**Signalkuppe 4556m**	102m
11.	Signalkuppe – E. ridge gendarme 4550m	15m
12.	Mont Blanc Petite Bosse 4547m	2m
13.	**Dom 4545m**	1018m
14.	Nordend S. ridge top 4542m	5m
15.	**Liskamm 4527m**	376m
16.	Mont Blanc Grande Bosse 4513m	5m
17.	**Weisshorn 4505m**	1055m
18.	Dufourspitze higher W. ridge summit 4499m	20m
19.	**Täschhorn 4490m**	209m
20.	Dom, western fore-summit 4479m	15m
21.	Liskamm west summit 4479m	62m
22.	**Matterhorn 4478m**	1164m
23.	Matterhorn west summit 4476m	15m
24.	Mont Blanc SW. ridge, Pic Luigi Amadeo 4469m	40m
25.	Dom, NE. ridge summit 4468m	15m
26.	**Mont Maudit 4465m**	162m
27.	Zumsteinspitze, SW. ridge top 4463m	15m
28.	Liskamm W. summit, E. fore-summit c.4450m	58m
29.	**Parrotspitze 4436m**	5m
30.	Täschhorn north ridge summit 4404m	136m
31.	Dufourspitze, lower W. ridge summit c.4385m	15m
32.	Weisshorn higher N. ridge top 4362m	25m
33.	**Dent Blanche 4356m**	15m
34.	Mont Maudit north-east summit 4336m	20m
35.	Liskamm E. shoulder (C.Scoperta) 4335m	10m

36.	Weisshorn N. ridge Gr. Gendarme 4331m	70m
37.	**Nadelhorn 4327m**	206m
38.	**Schwarzhorn 4322m**	50m
39.	**Grand Combin 4314m**	1517m
40.	**Ludwigshöhe 4311m**	897m
41.	Mont Blanc, Dôme du Goûter 4304m	58m
42.	Dufourspitze, lower W. ridge summit c.4280m	30m
43.	**Lenzspitze 4294m**	90m
44.	Liskamm, Naso 4273m	40m
45.	**Finsteraarhorn 4273m**	2108m
46.	Aiguille du Croissant 4250m	15m
47.	**Mont Blanc du Tacul 4248m**	213m
48.	Mont Blanc du Tacul E. summit 4247m	20m
49.	Mont Blanc S. ridge Gr. Pilier d'Angle 4243m	10m
50.	**Stecknadelhorn 4241m**	30m
51.	Pic Tyndall 4241m (Matterhorn)	15m
52.	**Castor 4228m**	165m
53.	**Zinalrothorn 4221m**	471m
54.	**Hohberghorn 4219m**	77m
55.	**Vincent Piramide 4215m**	128m
56.	**Grandes Jorasses 4208m**	843m
57.	**Alphubel 4206m**	355m
58.	Castor N. summit 4205m	5m
59.	Weisshorn, smaller N. ridge gendarme c.4205m	15m
60.	Weisshorn, lower N. ridge summit 4203m	30m
61.	Liskamm SW. ridge top 4201m	10m
62.	Zinalrothorn Kanzel c.4200m	15m
63.	**Rimpfischhorn 4199m**	410m
64.	**Aletschhorn 4195m**	1017m
65.	**Strahlhorn 4190m**	401m
66.	Alphubel N.summit 4188m	15m
67.	Castor, south-eastern fore-summit 4185m	10m
68.	Grand Combin de Valsorey 4184m	52m
69.	Pointe Whymper 4184m (Grandes Jorasses)	40m
70.	Weisshorn E. ridge tower 4178m	10m
71.	Täschhorn SE. ridge shoulder summit 4175m	10m
72.	Felikhorn 4174m (Castor)	10m
73.	**Dent d'Hérens 4171m**	692m
74.	**Balmenhorn 4167m**	12m
75.	Finsteraarhorn, SE. fore-summit 4167m	10m
76.	**Breithorn 4164m**	433m
77.	Breithorn, central summit 4159m	83m

78.	**Bishorn 4153m**	120m
79.	**Jungfrau 4158m**	684m
80.	Zinalrothorn Bosse (north ridge) c.4150m	15m
81.	Grand Combin de Tsessetta 4141m	55m
82.	Western Breithornzwilling 4139m	117m
83.	Pointe Burnaby 4135m (Bishorn)	25m
84.	**Aiguille Verte 4122m**	579m
85.	Zinalrothorn Gabelturm c.4120m	15m
86.	Isolée (P. Blanchard) 4114m (M.B. du Tacul)	36m
87.	**Aiguille Blanche (P. Güssfeldt) 4112m**	178m
88.	Mont Blanc du Tacul Pointe Carmen 4109m	54m
89.	Weisshorn lowest north ridge top 4109m	15m
90.	Rimpfischhorn north ridge gendarme 4108m	30m
91.	P. Androsace 4107m (M. Maudit SE. ridge)	10m
92.	P. Seymour King 4107m (Aig. Blanche S)	30m
93.	Eastern Breithornzwilling 4106m (Breithorn)	30m
94.	P. Jones 4104m (Aig. Blanche NW. summit)	15m
95.	**Grande Rocheuse 4102m**	70m
96.	**Barre des Écrins 4101m**	2043m
97.	Pointe Croz 4101m (Grandes Jorasses)	20m
98.	Zinalrothorn Sphinx c.4100m (N. ridge)	10m
99.	Tour Rouge c.4100m (M.B. du Tacul E. pillar)	20m
100.	**Mönch 4099m**	415m
101.	Dent Blanche Grand Gendarme 4098m (S. ridge)	8m
102.	Pointe Médiane 4097m (M.B. du Tacul)	40m
103.	Felikjoch top 4093m (east of Castor)	30m
104.	**Pollux 4092m**	247m
105.	Wengener Jungfrau 4089m	40m
106.	Finsteraarhorn NW. ridge top 4088m	10m
107.	Pic Lory 4086m (Barre des Écrins)	10m
108.	Aletschhorn NE. ridge top 4086m	8m
109.	**Schreckhorn 4078m**	788m
110.	Schwarzfluh/Roccia Nera 4075m (Breithorn)	15m
111.	P. Chaubert 4074m (M.B. du Tacul)	57m
112.	Aletschhorn WNW. ridge top 4071m	5m
113.	Mont Blanc du Tacul east face P.4067	20m
114.	Pointe Marguerite 4066m (Grandes Jorasses)	30m
115.	Corne du Diable 4064m (M.B. du Tacul)	17m
116.	**Obergabelhorn 4063m**	405m
117.	**Gran Paradiso 4061m**	1879m
118.	Gran Paradiso Madonna summit 4058m	7m
119.	**Mont Brouillard 4053m**	39m

120.	**Aiguille de Bionassay 4052m**	160m
121.	**Piz Bernina 4049m**	2234m
122.	**Gross-Fiescherhorn 4049m**	391m
123.	Punta Giordani 4046m	5m
124.	Pointe Hélene 4045m (Grandes Jorasses)	20m
125.	**Gross-Grünhorn 4044m**	305m
126.	**Lauteraarhorn 4042m**	128m
127.	Pic Eccles 4041m (Mont Blanc Innominata ridge)	15m
128.	Dent d'Hérens Épaule 4039m	20m
129.	**Aiguille du Jardin 4035m**	37m
130.	**Dürrenhorn 4035m**	119m
131.	**Allalinhorn 4027m**	265m
132.	Mont Blanc du Tacul east slope P.4027	20m
133.	Il Roc 4026m (Gran Paradiso east summit)	20m
134.	Pointe Eveline 4026m (Aiguille du Jardin)	5m
135.	Dufourspitze lowest W. ridge tower 4026m	20m
136.	**Hinter-Fiescherhorn 4025m**	102m
137.	**Weissmies 4023m**	1185m
138.	Pointe Croux 4023m (Aiguille Verte)	10m
139.	Bernina-Spalla 4020m	8m
140.	Zinalrothorn Épaule 4017m	5m
141.	**Dôme de Rochefort 4015m**	190m
142.	Gran Paradiso central summit 4015m	15m
143.	Dôme de Neige 4015m (Barre des Écrins)	25m
144.	**Dent du Géant 4013m**	139m
145.	**Punta Baretti 4013m**	56m
146.	Lauteraarhorn NW. ridge summit 4011m	10m
147.	**Lagginhorn 4010m**	511m
148.	Rimpfischhorn west summit 4009m	15m
149.	**Aiguille de Rochefort 4001m**	106m
150	**Les Droites 4000m**	204m

And now, if inclined, the reader can choose which of these elevations are significant enough for a visit to be worthwhile!

Graded List

The climbs listed by grades (but within each grade, in book order) plus the height-gain of the climb from the main hut. This sometimes includes an overnight stop (h) at a high intermediary hut. The grades assume ascents in optimum conditions. Some climbs on very high mountains have quite easy grades that belie their scale, remoteness and potential seriousness if the weather deteriorates – these are marked*. Other climbs have very long approaches to their base huts shown in the overall effort list on page 236.

D+

	climb length	page
Aiguille Blanche and over Mont Blanc	2217m (h)	222

D

Aiguille du Jardin	1400m	184

AD+

Schreckhorn	1558m	42
Lauteraarhorn	1550m	45
Täschhorn (either route) and traverse to Dom	1650m (h)	88
Grand Combin (North-West Face)	1450m	171

AD

Dürrenhorn/Hohberghorn/Nadelhorn	1500m	60
Lenzspitze (ENE Ridge and on to Nadelhorn)	1000m	82
Weisshorn	1600m	107
Obergabelhorn	850m	115
Dent Blanche	850m	117
Aiguille Verte (both routes)	1450m	176
Grande Rocheuse	1430m	183
Les Droites	1300m	185
Rochefort Ridge	1300m	192
Dent du Géant	730m	195
Aig. du Bionnassay and on to Gouter Route	1738m (h)	217
Mont Brouillard/Punta Baretti	800m	219

AD−

Zinalrothorn	1050m	111
Liskamm	920m	136
Matterhorn	1200m	162
Grandes Jorasses	1400m	187

PD+	climb length	page
Barre des Écrins	1000m	21
Aletschhorn (South-West Face)	1200m	26
Jungfrau	850m	30
Gross-Fiescherhorn	750m	36
Gross-Grünhorn	1400m	39
Rimpfischhorn	1600m	99
Dent d'Hérens	1400m	169
Grand Combin (West Ridge)	1300m	171
Mont Blanc (Gonella Route)	1736m*	205

PD		
Piz Bernina	1550m (h)	13
Aletschhorn (North-East Ridge)	1200m	26
Mönch	500m	34
Hinter-Fiescherhorn	750m	38
Finsteraarhorn	1300m	50
Lagginhorn	1280m/960m	54
Weissmies	1050m	58
Nadelhorn (North-East Ridge)	1000m	64
Lenzspitze (South-West Ridge)	1350m	82
Dom	1650m*	85
Alphubel	1330m	91
Allalinhorn (Hohlaubgrat)	1050m	95
Strahlhorn	1250m	103
Nordend	1820m*	120
Dufourspitze	1880m*	123
Signalkuppe plus (in various combinations)		
Zumsteinspitze / Ludwigshöhe /	1000m (h)	128
Parrotspitze / Schwarzhorn / Balmenhorn		
Vincent Piramide	600m	134
Castor	650m	139
Pollux	600m	141
Mont Blanc du Tacul	730m	197
Mont Maudit	1000m	201
Mont Blanc (Goûter Route)	1050m*	205

PD−/F		
Gran Paradiso	1350m	18
Allalinhorn (West Ridge)	580m	95
Bishorn	900m	105
Breithorn	350m	143
Mont Blanc (Grands Mulets Route)	1776m*	205

How much sweat?
Least ascent by ordinary route,
from the highest transport point.

1.	Dom	3160m
2.	Weisshorn	3100m
3.	Aiguille Blanche	2800m
4.	Zinalrothorn	2750m
5.	Schreckhorn	2720m
6.	Grand Combin	2700m
7.	Grandes Jorasses	2600m
8.	Mont Blanc	2550m
9.	Dent Blanche	2550m
10.	Obergabelhorn	2550m
11.	Bishorn	2480m
12.	Aiguille de Bionnassay	2400m
13.	Aiguille Verte	2350m
14.	Barre des Écrins	2350m
15.	Punta Baretti	(2350m)
16.	Täschhorn	2300m
17.	Grande Rocheuse	(2300m)
18.	Aiguille du Jardin	2300m
19.	Lenzspitze	2200m
20.	Dent d'Hérens	2200m
21.	Mont Brouillard	2200m
22.	Lauteraarhorn	2200m
23.	Les Droites	2200m
24.	Dufourspitze	2130m
25.	Nordend	2070m
26.	Gran Paradiso	2050m
27.	Nadelhorn	2000m
28.	Aletschhorn	2000m
29.	Matterhorn	1900m
30.	Finsteraarhorn	1800m
31.	Stecknadelhorn	(1800m)
32.	Hohberghorn	(1750m)
33.	Rimpfischhorn	1680m
34.	Dürrenhorn	(1600m)
35.	Piz Bernina	1550m
36.	Gross-Grünhorn	1500m
37.	Zumsteinspitze	(1300m)
38.	Signalkuppe	1300m

39.	Mont Maudit	1300m
40.	Dôme de Rochefort	1300m
41.	Liskamm	1270m
42.	Strahlhorn	1250m
43.	Parrotspitze	(1100m)
44.	Weissmies	1050m
45.	Aiguille de Rochefort	1050m
46.	Gross-Fiescherhorn	1050m
47.	Mont Blanc du Tacul	1030m
48.	Schwarzhorn	(1000m)
49.	Ludwigshöhe	(1000m)
50.	Vincent Piramide	(1000m)
51.	Hinter-Fiescherhorn	1000m
52.	Lagginhorn	960m
53.	Balmenhorn	(950m)
54.	Alphubel	860m
55.	Jungfrau	850m
56.	Dent du Géant	730m
57.	Pollux	700m
58.	Castor	600m
59.	Allalinhorn	580m
60.	Mönch	550m
61.	Breithorn	400m

Summits taken in conjunction with others are shown in parentheses.

Index

(page numbers)

Aar Bivouac 49
Adlerpass 103
Agüzza, Crast 15
Aiguille Blanche 222f
Aiguille du Jardin 184
Aiguille Verte 176f
Ailefroide 23
Alagna 129
Aletschhorn 25f
Aletschgletscher 25f
Allalinhorn 95f
Alphubel 91f
Androsace, Pointe 203
Anniviers, Val d' 105
Aosta 19
Aosta Hut 169
Arbengrat 116
Argentière-la-Bessée 23
Arolla 170, 174

Balmenhorn 133
Bäregg 43
Barre des Écrins 21f
Bellavista 15
Bernina, Piz 13f
Bettmeralp 27
Bionnassay, Aiguille 217f
Bishorn 105f
Blanchard, Pointe 199
Blatten 27
Boccalatte Hut 189
Bosse (Zinalroth.) 114
Bosses (M. Blanc) 213
Bossongletscher 212
Bourg-St-Pierre 172
Breithorn 143f
Breithornzwillinge 161
Brenva, Col de la 203
Brenva Face 207, 216
Breuil 159
Bricola, Alpe 117
Britannia Hut 96, 104
Burnaby, Pointe 106

Carmen, Pointe 199
Castor 139f
Cervinia 159
Cesare e G. Hut 144

Cézanne Hut 23
Chamonix 179
Chaubert, Pointe 199
Chüebodenstafel 39
Città Mantova Hut 129
Couergrat 116
Combin Tsessetta 177
Combin Valsorey 177
Corne du Diable 199
Courmayeur 189
Cour., M.Blanc de 213
Couvercle Hut 180f
Craveri Bivouac 226
Croissant, Aig. du 175
Croux, Pointe 182
Croz, Pointe 190

Dent Blanche 117f
Dent Blanche Hut 18
Dent d'Hérens 169f
Dent du Géant 195
Diavolezza 14
Dom 85f
Dôme de Neige 24
Dôme de Rochefort 196
Dôme du Goûter 210f
Dom Hut 84, 86, 88
Droites, Les 185f
Dufourspitze 123f
Durance 22
Durier Hut 218
Dürrenhorn 60f

Écrin Hut 23
Eccles, Pic 216
Eggishorn 39
Eismeer 43
Épaule (Dt. d'Hér.) 170
Épaule (Zinalroth.) 114
Eveline, Pointe 184
Ewigschneeefeld 36, 38

Feechopf 94
Feejoch 94, 96
Felikhorn 140
Felikjoch-Kuppe 140
Festi-Kin-Lucke 90
Festijoch 86
Fiesch 30, 39f
Fieschersattel 37f
Finsteraarhorn 50f
Finsteraarhorn Hut 37ff

Flue, Berggasthaus 101
Franscia 14, 16

Gaagg 44
Gabelgrat 116
Gandegg Hut 144
Giacomo, San 139,142
Giordani, Punta 135
Glacier Blanc Hut 23
Gnifetti Hut 129
Gonella Hut 216
Gornergletscher 122f
Gornergratbahn 120f
Goûter, Aiguille du 208f
Goûter, Dôme du 210f
Grafeney, Combin 171f
Graham, Pointe 195
Graian Alps 18
Gran Paradiso 18
Grand Combin 171f
Grand Pilier d'Angle 213
Grande Chandelle 213
Grande Rocheuse 183
Grandes Jorasses 187f
Grand Mulets Hut 212
Grenzgipfel 126
Gressoney 139
Grimselhospiz 46
Grindlewald 32, 43
Grises, Aiguilles 208
Gross-Fiesherhorn 36
Gross-Grunhorn 39f
Gruber, Rochers 224, 228
Grüneggfirn 51
Grünegghorn 39f
Grünhornlücke 49
Guggi Hut 35
Güssfeldt, Pointe 228

Hannigalpe 81
Haudères, Les 117
Hélène, Pointe 190
Hérens, Dent d' 169
Hérens, Val de 117
Hirondelles Ridge 190
Hinter-Fiescherhorn 38
Hohbalmgletscher 62
Hohberghorn 60,79
Hohlaubgrat 96
Hohsaas 54, 58
Hörnli Ridge 166f
Hugisattel 52

Il Roc 20
Isolée 199

Jones, Pointe 228
Jungfrau 30f
Jungfraufirn 31

Konkordia Huts 36, 40
Konkordiaplatz 39
Kranzbergegg 33
Kreuzboden 59
Kuffnergrat 204

Lac Combal 218
Lagginhorn 54f
Langflue 92
Langfluejoch 101
Lauteraargletscher 48
Lauteraar Hut 48
Lauteraarhorn 45f
Lenzspitze 82f
Liongrat 167
Liskamm 136f
Ludwigshöhe 134

Marco e Rosa Huts 14f
Marghérita Hut 128
Marguerite, Pointe 190
Märjensee 27, 40
Matterhorn 162f
Médiane, Pointe 199
Meitin, Col du 171f
Mezzalama Hut 142
Miage, Col de 218
Miage Glacier 212, 217f
Midi, Aiguille du 197
Mischabel 60f
Mischabel Huts 81, 83
Mittelaletsch Biv. 27
Mittelallalin 91, 96
Moine ridge 180
Mönch 34f
Mönchsjoch Hut 31f
Mont Brouillard 221f
Mont Maudit 210f
Mont Blanc 176f, 205f
Mt. Bl. de Cour. 213
Monte Rosa Hut 127f
Montenvers 180
Monzino Hut 224
Morteratsch 14
Montets Hut 112, 116

Nadelgrat 60
Nadelhorn 60, 80f
Nordend 120

Oberaletsch Hut 27
Obergabelhorn 115

Pannossière Hut 171
Parrotspitze 131
Peuterey Ridge 216
Pfulwe 101
Pic Eccles 213
Pic Lory 24
Pic Luigi Amedeo 213
Pic Tyndall 187f
Piz Bernina 13f
Planpancieux 189
Pollux 141f
Pont 19
Pontresina 14
Prarayer 169
Punta Baretti 219
Punta Inddren 129, 136

Randa 85, 109
Reposoir Rocks 189
Rey, Cresta 126
Rimpfischhorn 99
Roccia Nera 161
Rochefort, Aig. de 192
Rothorn Hut 112
Rottalsattel 31f
Rossier Hut 118

Saas Fee 80, 93
Saas Grund 58
St Gervais 217
Savaranche, Val 19
Schneedomspitze 138
Schönbiel Hut 169
Schreckhorn 42f
Schreckhorn Hut 43
Schwarzfluh 161
Schwarzhorn 133
Schwarzsee 165
Scoperta, Cima 138
Sella Bivouac 220
Sella Hut 140
Sella, Pointe 195
Seymour King, Pte 228
Signalkuppe 128f
Silbersattel 121

Spalla (Bernina) 17
Sphinx 114
Sphinxstollen 31, 34
Stecknadelhorn 60, 79
Stieregg 43
Strahlhorn 103f
Sunegga 100

Täätsche 27
Tacul, M. Blanc du 197f
Talèfre, Glacier de 180
Täsch 91, 124
Täschhorn 88f
Täsch Hut 102
Theodule Hut 160
Testa Grigia 159
Teufelsgrat (Tacul) 200
Teufelsgrat (Täsch) 94
Torino Hut 192
Tour Rouge 200
Tracuit Hut 106
Tresse 217
Tricot Ridge 218
Trift Hotel 112
Triftjigrat 161

Vallot Hut 210
Valpelline 169
Valsorey Hut 171
Veni, Val 214
Vincent Piramide 134
Vitt. Emanuele II Hut 19

Walker Spur 188, 190
Wandfluegrat 118
Weingartengletscher 92
Weisshorn 107f
Weisshorn Hut 110
Weissmies 56f
Weissmies Huts 55f
Weisstor 104
Wellenkuppe 115f
Wengener Jungfrau 33
Whymper Couloir 180f
Whymper, Pointe 190
Windjoch 81

Zermatt 100, 112, 123f
Zinal 109
Zinalrothorn 115f
Zumsteinspitze 127
Zwillingsjoch 142

A Note on Rock Climbing Grades and Training

The UIAA rock climbing grading scale converts as follows:

UIAA	British	American
I	Moderate	5.1-5.2
II	Difficult	5.2-5.3
III	Very Difficult	5.4
IV	Severe	5.5
V	Very Severe	5.6-5.7
VI	Hard Very Severe	5.8-5.9

It is well to maintain a healthy respect for alpine rock pitches. This simple conversion table fails to make the point that the rock pitches on the 4000 metre peaks must be tackled when heavily accoutred in boots (sometimes in crampons), anoraks and with heavy sacs. Pitches are often wet, iced, snow-covered or loose and may have to be climbed in dawn light when the rock is clammy and cold, or during inclement weather. The climber's performance may be reduced by fatigue or weakness brought on by altitude. For all these reasons, alpine rock climbing difficulties cannot be compared to similarly graded climbs on valley crags.

To prepare for such a 'culture' shock, it is well to spend a few hard days of simulated alpine climbing – 'boots and sacs days' on a selection of your favourite climbs – before setting out for the alps. When you reach your alpine destination a further half day of glacier and snow training is always valuable (even for experienced teams). This would include cramponing and ice axe technique (particularly braking involuntary slips) glacier belaying, crevasse rescue and alpine rope techniques. The final obvious precaution is to start with an undemanding training climb to allow all these techniques to be perfected, to ascertain the fitness of each member of the party and to tune up the habits of speedy movement.

The following technique books are useful:

Handbook of Climbing by Allen Fyffe and Iain Peter
Pelham Books (London)

Glacier Travel and Crevasse Rescue by Andy Selters
The Mountaineers (Seattle) and Diadem Books (London)

Avalanche Safety for Skiers and Climbers by Tony Daffern
Rocky Mountain Books (Calgary) and Diadem Books (London)